CRACKING
THE
DATA CODE

Unlock the
hidden value of data
for your organisation

MIKE BUGEMBE

R3THINK PRESS

First published in Great Britain in 2018 by
Rethink Press (www.rethinkpress.com)

Cover image @ Shutterstock/sdecoret

Contents

Introduction

Data has become the most exciting and disruptive force in our world. Today's vast quantities of data, and unprecedented access to it, are being used to fundamentally improve every aspect of our lives. Data is effectively making us smarter, healthier and safer. It's used to improve our public and private lives as well as our environment. Companies are using it to produce new and innovative data-driven goods, services and business models. They're also developing new approaches to every internal business function, from operations to recruitment and employee engagement. Quite frankly, every aspect of our world has benefited from this, which shows that there is absolutely no reason data can't be a game changer for you and your organisation.

It would be irresponsible, though, not to acknowledge that these big, game-changing opportunities are also coupled with ethical challenges, arising primarily from the ever-increasing volume of personal and sometimes sensitive data to which companies have access. Fortunately, bodies like the Information Commission in the UK have been created to uphold the information rights of individuals and ensure consumer safety while simultaneously encouraging corporations to continue with data innovations in an ethical and transparent way. With these safeguards in place, corporations continue to use data to improve our lives in many ways, such as expanding the opportunities for charitable giving, predicting food shortages and preventing famine, and even identifying and addressing various forms of corruption.

Imagine a world in which you have an in-depth understanding of what's happening in your complex business environment – or better still, you're able to understand *why* it happened. You understand why sales suddenly dropped, why your users drastically changed their engagement, or why you are not growing as fast as you had forecast. Data helps answer these questions and much more. With data, companies can move from understanding not only *what* and *why* things happened, to *predicting* what is likely to happen, algorithmically *prescribing* the most effective action and even using artificial intelligence (AI) to take on the next action with no human intervention.

The opportunity that data presents is, quite frankly, undeniable.

WHO CAN BENEFIT FROM DATA?

Organisations that successfully use data typically experience exceptional growth and financial benefits, establishing themselves as market leaders in their respective industries. Naturally, when we consider organisations that use data, we think of the Googles, Amazons and Facebooks of this world, where time, effort and investment in extracting value through data mining has resulted in billion-dollar valuations and market dominance.

While these are great examples, I have also seen how using these companies as case studies creates the mistaken belief that to realise the game-changing benefits that data promises, your company must be a mega-organisation with an abundance of technical resources and origins in Silicon Valley. This is simply not true. It's a notion that must be debunked.

Today, the benefits derived from data have been democratised and every organisation – including yours – can ignore the barriers of size, budget and industry. We tend to think only of technical organisations when it comes to data success stories, but consider the following examples in non-technical – even somewhat traditional – industries:

- Leading sports teams predict and prevent the onset of injury, prolonging the life and efficiency of their players

- The world of health and medicine is using predictive data algorithms to identify the onset of certain conditions such as depression, which enables practitioners to address them preventatively, moving away from traditional expensive, resource-intensive, reactive approaches

- Intelligence agencies are preventing devastating terrorist activity by using data to determine where to deploy units before an attack takes place

As a leader in your organisation, you'll inevitably have to consider how you can get data to work for your organisation. How more specifically you can use data to increase market share, super charge growth, create competitive advantage, grow and find new sources of revenue or employ a more internal focus on identifying operational efficiencies, like increasing quality, productivity and employee retention. The list, simply goes on and on.

Even at its very basic level, data will give you invaluable insights into all the constituents that add value to your organisation, such as the employees, customers and suppliers. You can get never-before-seen insights into their behaviours and personal preferences

– which can be used to create new products, person-alise services or streamline your operations to drive transformational business models, increase revenue, growth, innovation and productivity. When your organisation becomes more data savvy, your insights can move from an understanding of what is happening and why, to predicting what is going to happen and using machine learning and AI to prescribe the best solution and find winning strategies to achieve your organisation's key objectives.

To realise these benefits and more, all leaders in all departments or business units of any organisations, irrespective of industry, will have no choice but to invest in data.

THE COST OF IGNORING DATA

The cost of avoiding this investment in data can be severe. Organisations that fail to see the opportunity and delay the start of their data journey are at serious risk of being leapfrogged by more data-savvy com-petitors. It's a mistake to assume your competitors are not actively seeking ways to win with data. I would bet my house on the fact that at least one executive in every Fortune 500 company has recognised the need to harness value from data and establish it as a pillar of their strategy to grow and achieve market dominance.

The risk of ignoring data while your competitors reap game-changing rewards before you do is too high to ignore. This means that all twenty-first-century organisations, regardless of industry, face the same challenge and are asking themselves these questions:

- How do we get data to work for our organisation?

- How do we create clear, tangible value for all constituents from unprecedented access to so much data?

- How do we use data to stimulate the new cutting edge of business innovation?

- Can we predict what the future of our industry will look like so that we can start planning and move first?

WHY MANY FAIL WITH DATA

The harsh reality is that many who start working on a data initiative invest a large amount of time, resources and effort – yet, sadly, are destined to fail. A survey from 2015 found that only 8% of leaders are fully satisfied with their big data and data science initiatives,[1] while another survey shows that 92% of organisations have failed to achieve lift-off or are

---

1   www.datanami.com/2015/02/04/survey-finds-uneven-success-big-data-rollouts

stuck in neutral.[2] Unfortunately, the statistics are not in your favour, and if you follow in the footsteps of these organisations your investment will most likely fail to see a return.

Given that we are living in the information age, with vast quantities and varieties of data available, we must ask ourselves: Why is it that companies that can access much of this data still fail to benefit from it?

When investing in data and beginning to seek value from it, most organisations go no further than the recruitment of a what is commonly referred to as a data science (DS) team – a highly technical team packed with PhD-level analysts who have the ability to write complex data algorithms. Sadly, this is not enough.

Data delivers value to the business by working *with* the business, not in isolation. No executive would leave it to a purely technical team to negotiate the delicate balance between consumer needs and profitability, or profit per customer versus growth in market share. Since value can be realised from data across the *entire* organisation, and the decision on where to focus the data efforts is crucial, success calls for more than commitment from the executive leadership team: it needs full involvement!

---

2   www.informationweek.com/big-data/big-data-analytics/8-reasons-big-data-projects-fail/a/d-id/1297842

Sadly, this is where the key barriers to exploiting data successfully typically materialise. Many business users do not even understand what data really is and will struggle to articulate clearly what it is used for. If you were to pick several executives randomly from a range of companies and ask them to define data, what it is used for and what a data scientist (DS) is, you will get different answers. This issue is not restricted to non-technical executives; there is a lot of data jargon out there and even the so-called experts fail to agree on much of the existing terminology. This will have a direct impact on your game plan for data, hiring strategy and any initiatives designed to create a data-driven culture.

This means that most companies are unable to fully appreciate and use the data that they have access to effectively. Few have the technical ability, resources, time and tools to take apart, mine and analyse data to identify and realise its benefits. Fewer still have business executives with the right values, behaviours and disciplines to get data really working for them.

Put simply, organisations in general have a data competency issue in their executive leadership teams.

Generating value from data can be a complex journey, with many small and specific moving parts and dependent sequences that must be understood and mastered. As a result, many have found that using data successfully is not all about the statistics, or about the number of PhDs you employ, or the amount of data that you have. Business value from data cannot be unlocked if the enterprise is limited to the efforts of the technical analytical team. Instead, as with any team sport, success from data will require the attention of most of the organisation and will impact the organisational, structural and behavioural aspects of the entire company.

UNRAVELLING THE DATA PUZZLE

With this myriad of complexity and test of ingenuity, the challenge of generating the game-changing value that data promises is best described as a puzzle in which missing pieces distort the picture such that, in effect, the puzzle remains unsolved.

When I started my journey with data, I found little documentation on this puzzle and how to solve it, so I set out to find a solution, get it to work, simplify it and document it. I spent eight years studying and working with organisations that seemed to have solved this puzzle: from the large tech data giants such as Facebook and Google to smaller ones that had found a way to get it to work. I also spent time with those that failed to realise the benefits that data promises. During this research period a clear set of ingredients, values and behaviours emerged among the successful organisations that were generally absent from those that were not successful.

I took time to model, develop and codify that pattern into an approach – an algorithm if you like – that can be used to substantially increase your chances of success with data. I was able to put the process to test with a range of clients and was fortunate enough to see them join the short list of companies that are experiencing the game-changing success that data promises.

My biggest personal success was during my time as the chief analytics officer at JustGiving.com, a small British-based company that serves the online needs of charity fundraisers. The innovative, data-driven, smart products that my team built were among the key reasons for the $100,000,000 acquisition of the company – the biggest acquisition of a tech company operating in the non-profit space – creating a few millionaires in the process. We built intelligent algorithms that could understand and learn what givers were passionate about, when they preferred to give, how much they were willing to donate, and how best to engage with them to maximise the chance of follow-through with a generous act. These machine-learning algorithms generated millions of pounds for the charities and causes that people are passionate about and was a key component of the acquisition and strategy, going forward.

This process of working with data to generate innovative, market-dominating value from the vast quantities of data available is what this book is about. It's a relatively complex process, but my mission has been to simplify it and, in doing so, I've rolled up all the key components, actions, values and behaviours into five distinct keys to cracking the data code:

1. An organisational understanding of what data is and how it delivers value

2. A qualified data leader

3. A strategic game plan

4. A competent, diverse team

5. A data-driven organisational culture

Each of the following chapters explores these components in detail, providing practical examples and guidance for how to embed them in your organisation.

WHY YOU NEED THIS BOOK

Every organisation, regardless of industry or size, has a data puzzle that they can solve. Each puzzle has a unique picture, a unique end game and a unique vision each as distinctive as a fingerprint. Among this sea of eccentric idiosyncrasies lies a common cross-industry approach to solving the puzzle. These five keys may seem simple enough, but there is a high degree of complexity when you dive into each one.

For example, can the leaders of your organisation explain what data is? Do they understand the difference between the popular cousins of data science – machine learning and AI – as well as what data is actually used for? Can *you* provide a robust response to these issues? What are the characteristics of the data leader that you should appoint? Should that person sit with the leadership team or report to IT? Can you succeed by recruiting only DSs? What are the visible behaviours and attitudes that make you a data-driven company poised to find that perfect use case for data?

When looking at the recruitment of your data leader, do you know what he or she is supposed to do, and what deliverables you should expect? Is this person going to recruit a team to execute the mission? Are you on the same page with the plan, going forward?

These questions represent only the tip of the iceberg of unknowns that must be understood and answered at a leadership level. While the five main keys for success may seem simple, there are indeed deep layers of complexity to each that must be understood.

Many organisations believe that they have these five keys to success in place, yet they fail to see results. This is because data closely resembles the algorithms that use it: two companies can produce an algorithm to identify which customers to promote a new offer to, but the details of the algorithm and the data used to train and test it are where the differences lie.

To make data work for you, there is no choice but to understand the nuances in each of these five components, irrespective of the size or nature of your organisation. Doing this has allowed me to demonstrate that organisations that take time to invest correctly in the process of generating value from data will achieve their goals and objectives, experience revenue growth and profitability and increase their chances of dominating their industry verticals.

Who this book is for

With media buzz around data success stories like JustGiving.com, data-related terms are now popular buzzwords in the business world. But how many C-suite executives and line managers (except for those with advanced degrees in computer science or mathematics) know what data or its close cousins of data science – AI and analytics – truly are? More importantly, how many know exactly what they need to do to extract true value from data? As a leader in your organisation, do you?

As my friend and fellow author Graham Hogg describes it, 'data is a team sport' and, in this case, the team consists of most people in the organisation, from C-level executives to the developer writing code or the customer service rep assisting users with their queries. Therefore, the ultimate key to solving data lies not only with an understanding of the ingredients, nor is it a case of simply having each ingredient in place. It boils down to leadership and can't be delegated to IT professionals or programmers alone.

With data as the fuel for business innovation, disrupting every industry and creating new opportunities in all parts of the business, each leader around the table essentially has an opportunity for data to work specifically for them and their respective areas. Thomas H Davenport, co-author of *Competing on Analytics: The New Science of Winning*, says, 'The entry barrier is no longer technology, but whether you have executives who understand this.'

When you consider the five key ingredients, you'll notice that the leadership team has an active role to play in each of them. They must understand the definitions to be part of the solution. They will need to work with and ensure that the appointed data leader has the tools required to succeed. Unless the leadership team understands what's required, the wrong leader will be appointed and/or will be positioned incorrectly within the organisation, resulting in an inability to deliver.

The game plan may indeed involve each leader's own personal areas of responsibility. Often, the most exciting and impactful use cases for data do not come from the data leader, but from those who understand the requisite key strategic and corporate-level decisions. A lack of understanding of these things can result in the wrong team appointments and, probably most importantly, a non-supportive (although well-meaning) culture.

Remembering that data is a team sport, the appointed data leader can't change the culture of the organisation if the leadership does not exhibit the values and responsibilities that they wish the rest of the organisation to employ. Do you as a leader have a firm grasp of the values, beliefs and behaviours that are required from each of your employees and team members?

Today, organisations need analytically savvy managers capable of discovering patterns and finding relationships in complex data. They also need senior leaders who 'get it' –who have taken time to understand how to play their part in success. This especially includes the data leader appointed to execute this initiative – the one who is solely responsible for the delivery of game-changing value to your organisation.

This book will serve as an actionable handbook for you and the rest of your leadership team so that you are all on the same page with what data can do for your organisation. The five keys to success described here are what separates successful organisations from those that fail. I've learned this from my years of intense study and nearly two decades of experience in this realm.

The main audiences for this guide (executive leadership team, savvy managers and the data initiative lead) are not overly technical, so this is not a technical book. There are plenty of books on the market that cover the wide array of technical details on algorithm building, harnessing data and cloud mechanics, written for the mathematicians or DSs who create the equations or the technical teams that productionise those algorithms through code.

Instead, this is a *strategic* guide that brings to life the key requirements of a successful strategy for the management audience: business leaders who are excited about the possibility of cracking the data code and who are keen to realise the benefits at a corporate level – business leaders who ultimately will sponsor this work and make many of the key corporate-level decisions required for success.

If you are running a business, this book is for you. If you are the chief financial officer (CFO), the chief information officer (CIO) or even the chief marketing officer (CMO), then this book is for you as well, since all of you will play a part in either making data succeed or fail in your organisation. If you are a manager wishing to understand what to share with your leadership about data, this book is for you. If you have been blessed with the honour of leading this initiative, this will be your playbook.

An army of brilliant DSs with an absence of data-savvy organisational managers and leaders is a recipe for failure.

The next generation of industry leaders is inevitably going to need a combination of data science and management skills. I have written this book to show those leaders why they should care, and how they can prepare and execute a winning strategy to realise the extraordinary benefits that data promises.

I sincerely hope that you enjoy reading this book as much as I enjoyed writing it. Cracking the data code will help you and your organisation better serve your customers, become more efficient operationally, innovate more effectively, increase revenues and so much more.

In other words, the approach outlined in this book can help you and your organisation to achieve your strategic goals.

KEY #1
Demystifying Data

To build an organisational understanding of data we need to understand what data is, what we can do with it and where to apply it. These are the three important pillars that build a comprehensive understanding of data and, more importantly, they create the foundation for how to generate value from data. However, the challenge that we face is that the world of data has grown so fast that it is littered with complex terminology that makes an understanding of the three pillars incredibly difficult.

In early 2015, I attended a conference on big data. Shortly afterwards, I attended an AI summit, then ended the year at an evening function on data science. I noticed that there were four individual speakers who, by coincidence, spoke at each of those events.

What was less of a coincidence, but perhaps more interesting, is that each speaker did little to alter his or her presentation in each situation. In most cases, each delivered the exact same presentation, word for word and slide for slide. Does this mean that big data, data science and machine learning are all the same thing?

Often, when you hear people talk about data, you also hear the terms 'big data', 'data science', 'machine learning', 'Internet of things' and 'artificial intelligence'. These terms are frequently used interchangeably, even though they each play a different but important role in bringing to life the true potential of the data revolution.

I was leading a small workshop of about fifteen people and decided to ask them what each of these terms meant. In most cases, they bundled them all together to mean the same thing, illustrating that most of the new terminology around data is not clearly understood. Most people, including executives and individuals who call themselves experts, are not able to tell you the differences between them. This makes it difficult for executives to join the conversation, causing organisations to hire the wrong individuals and fail to compile strong data strategies or execute the strategies that they produce. Without knowing the differences between these key terms, how will you understand what to do to get the most out of data?

Therefore, we must start by providing concise definitions for the important and popular terms around data. To ensure that you can join the conversation, leaders, managers and even recruitment agents, will need to focus on being able to understand and explain these key terms:

- data

- big data

- cloud computing

- distributed computing

- analytics

- data science

- AI

- machine learning

- data engineering

For definitions of these terms, we must look back to when the world of IT chose the word 'mining' to describe what organisations should do with data, which I found to be an excellent analogy. Having spent five years leading the data initiative for a large diamond-mining company in the early 2000s, I was introduced to the high-level value chain for mined materials, which contained four key areas of focus:

1. Raw materials

2. Storage and processing

3. Processing procedures

4. Specific techniques used in the various processing procedures

To address the complex array of terms and definitions in data, I borrow heavily from these concepts and apply them directly to all key concepts in the world of data. When working with data, just as with mining for diamonds, there are raw elements that must be harvested and stored in a location ready for processing, and then put through a specific process, employing specific techniques according to purpose.

Throughout this chapter, I will explore each of the four categories in depth, to help demystify the complex language that plays a significant role in the success or failure of organisational data initiatives. This will equip executives and non-technical people from all walks of business – from marketing through recruitment and management – with the knowledge required to join the conversation.

RAW MATERIALS

In the value chain for data, as with any valuable product that is sourced from nature, we start with the material in its rawest form. In today's business scenario, two terms make up our raw material: 'data' and 'big data'.

Understanding data

The term 'data' is generally the most understood term on our list. Webster's Dictionary simply defines data as 'factual information (as measurements or statistics) used as a basis for reasoning, discussion, or calculation'.

Data has been around since the beginning of time; it's all around us in many forms. The colour of the trees outside is data. The speed of the wind that you feel brushing your face on a windy day is data. The temperature of the water at the beach is data.

All of these are forms of data that are stored and processed by our brains. Nature started the process of storing and recording data, keeping notes on key events that occurred in the past. Dendrochronology, the study of data from tree ring growth, is an example of this. Eventually, humans also began to store and record data, starting with cave paintings, tree carvings and hieroglyphics, and moving quickly on to books. Eventually, we started to store data digitally.

While the older methods of capturing data have not disappeared, most data today is captured and stored in a computer as a collection of numbers represented as bytes that are in turn composed of bits (binary digits) with values of 1 or 0. Computers can store a range of types of data such as visual images, sounds, text and encryption. It's this combination of increased digitisation of process, resulting in increased capture of data and the rapidly declining costs of storage, that has led to the explosion of what is now commonly referred to as 'big data'.

Understanding big data

Finding a consistent definition for 'big data' is difficult. The term seems to have morphed into a catch-all for anything to do with data, including the process of collecting it, storing it, analysing it or building products that use it – hence the notion that you can somehow 'do' big data. From my perspective, you need not be an English scholar to know that you cannot 'do' big data.

The trusted English Oxford Living Dictionary aligns with my thinking, defining big data as 'extremely large data sets that may be analysed computationally to reveal patterns, trends and associations, especially relating to human behaviour and interactions'. Despite a clear dictionary definition, confusion prevails, as big data is abused as a marketing buzzword.

A clear example of this can be seen in a simple experiment carried out by a team at UC Berkeley School of Information, who set out to settle the question once and for all: 'What is big data?'

One would have hoped that experts in the field would arrive at a consistent definition that we could all adopt but, sadly, that didn't happen. I analysed the responses from all forty-three experts and discovered some surprising and interesting facts.

Roughly 10% of the answers were quite philosophical. For example, Deirdre Mulligan of UC Berkeley School of Information described big data as 'endless possibilities or cradle-to-grave shackles, depending upon the political, ethical, and legal choices we make.' Drew Conway, Head of Data from Project Florida, offered this definition: 'Big data, which started as a technological innovation in distributed computing, is now a cultural movement by which we continue to discover how humanity interacts with the world – and each other – at large scale.'

More generally, though, the results showed that there are typically two schools of thought around what big data is. Some described big data as an activity, an approach or a process, while others described it as a thing, an item or an entity.

About 33% of the definitions described big data as an activity. I've picked out several examples, starting with Peter Skomoroch, entrepreneur and former principal DS at LinkedIn, who wrote: 'Big data originally described the practice in the consumer Internet industry of applying algorithms to increasingly large amounts of disparate data to solve problems that had suboptimal solutions with smaller datasets.'

Philip Ashlock from Data.gov said: 'While the use of the term is quite nebulous and is often co-opted for other purposes, I've understood "big data" to be about analysis for data that's really messy or where you don't know the right questions or queries to make — analysis that can help you find patterns, anomalies, or new structures amidst otherwise chaotic or complex data points...'

My final example is from Hilary Mason, the founder of Fast Forward Labs, who describes big data as 'the ability to gather information and query it in such a way that we are able to learn things about the world that were previously inaccessible to us'.

For these experts, big data is a process – one that entails the gathering and analysis of data and the application of algorithms. Describing big data in this way is not helpful because one could ask: 'If big data is a process, what then are analytics, machine learning and data science?'

The remaining 53% of experts described big data as what it says on the tin: big data is data, but there is just a lot of it. The chief economist at Google describes big data as 'data that cannot fit easily into a standard relational database'. Annette Greinier, lecturer at UC Berkeley School of Information, describes big data as 'data that contains enough observations to demand unusual handling because of its sheer size'.

My perspective is closely aligned with the 53% majority of the expert opinions from the UC Berkeley study. Big data cannot be a process; it is simply a lot of data – a plethora of facts about an activity, event, environment or situation. Sales figures, accident records and the temperature are all examples of data. It can comprise either qualitative or quantitative variables that have always existed, it's just that today more of it is captured and stored.

'Data' and 'big data' are the only terms that can be used interchangeably as they actually mean the same thing. The term 'big data' simply acknowledges the volume of data available today. As a result, you will see me use big data more than data throughout this text as it is inevitable that the volume of data will continue to grow. However, there is more to big data than the volume of data produced. To capture the true essence of big data, we must acknowledge other 'big' attributes of data today.

The three 'Vs' of big data

Doug Laney, a Gartner analyst, coined a more multidimensional description of big data that has garnered a lot of traction in recent years. His definition describes big data using three Vs:

- Volume: amount of data

- Variety: range of data types and sources

- Velocity: speed of data in and out

Since his definition, a range of other Vs have been introduced, but they only add to the complexity of what should be a simple and concise definition. I will therefore focus on understanding Laney's original three Vs.

Volume

Volume, as we have already established, refers to the amount of data that's being produced. A full 90% of the data in the world today has been generated in the last two years. Organisations are awash with data, easily accumulating terabytes of it that they cannot fit in standard machines or in traditional databases and that they cannot analyse as they did a decade ago. Today, so much more data is being captured because of a combination of factors including decreasing costs of data storage, ever-increasing capacity (which is doubling every two years in accordance with Kryder's Law), new applications and technology and changes in general human behaviour. Nearly all our daily activities and general interactions with each other pass through some sort of processor.

To compound that further, with the growth of the Internet of things – in which everyday objects have network capability, allowing them to send and receive data – we are expecting over 30 billion connected devices by 2020. Ubiquitous devices such as security cameras, handheld scanners, tablets, mobile phones, wireless sensors and many others are capturing an incredible amount of data. With the burden of capture and storage being eased by technology, we'll continue to see an explosion in the amount of data being transmitted and stored. This growing volume of data includes a growing *variety* of data.

Variety

The variety of data that we can now capture is one of the most exciting aspects of big data for me. It arrives in the form of unstructured text documents, images, audio and video – which means that we now have access to so much that wasn't available before. This widening of the scope of what is captured is fundamentally changing industries, disrupting traditional business and saving lives.

Take, for example, the humble diaper. It has always performed the function of allowing babies to urinate without soiling their outer clothing or contaminating the external environment. Data (or facts, information and evidence) on the frequency, colour and smell of babies' urine has been available in a medical setting, but difficult to capture at home in real time. With advances in today's sensor technology, that data can be collected, allowing real-time diagnosis of a baby's health by analysing the urine and informing parents of babies' levels of hydration and kidney health, among other things.

Typically, data like this would fall into the category of 'machine-generated data': data from industrial equipment, for example the several terabytes of data produced by the latest generation of aircraft on a single transatlantic flight, or real-time data from sensors on your smartphone or heart rate monitor, not to mention data from the millions of CCTV cameras and web logs that track user behaviours online.

Other varieties include good old-fashioned 'transactional data', but now with an exponential increase in data from invoices, payment orders, purchases, storage records, delivery records and the like. More recently, we have seen a significant increase in what's commonly called 'social data' coming from social media services such as Facebook, Twitter, YouTube and others. Social data also describes significant changes in our behaviours.

And, increasingly, we are making use of this data. We use devices to monitor our movements – when we exercise, where we drive our cars, and even when and how we eat and sleep. We track this data and share it more readily than ever before. We're also sharing our feelings and key personal moments in our lives.

We capture and share this wider variety of data so frequently that we contribute to the third big attribute of big data: velocity.

Velocity

The final V represents the rate at which data is produced. Consider the fact that Facebook users upload more than 900 million photos a day, or the vast number of tweets, status changes, videos uploaded, messages sent or even the number of credit card transactions taking place in any given period.

At any moment, millions of people the world over are generating an insane amount of data. The best estimate I found was from IBM in 2013. They claimed that, each day, we create over 2.5 quintillion bytes of data – that's eighteen zeros! – and that was several years ago. That should give you a healthy appreciation for the rate at which data is being created.

Much of what we do and many of our interactions with each other are through some form of technology, digital process or social media exchange, which all produce data. It's being produced in astronomical quantities, from a range of sources, at an alarming speed.

While many experts in the study mentioned previously described big data as an approach to capturing, processing and analysing data, I maintain that big data is the essential *ingredient*; the raw material for the processes that they describe.

To handle this raw material, we need new technology to ingest, store, process, file and, at some point, retrieve it all.

STORAGE AND PROCESSING

We have two challenges: where to store such large amounts of data, and how to run calculations on it. So, the next category of terms to examine are the ones that relate to storage and processing.

Data streams in at an unprecedented pace and must be processed in a timely manner. Traditional, static methods are not able to manage data produced at this rate. Building production systems to capture and store this amount of data demands a different set of skills, as well as a new set of systems to retrieve it and use it in complex calculations in real time. RFID (radio frequency identification) tags, sensors and smart metering are driving the need to deal with torrents of data in near real time.

Back in the 1970s, we needed big centralised mainframe systems to do our calculations and store our data. When personal computers took off, we could hire the services of a data-processing company with its own expensive computer systems that specialised in 'number crunching'. Today, we can do many of those mainframe jobs ourselves. Calculations, exploration and analysis can all be done easily on our desktops with off-the-shelf software, and the ability to store large amounts of data is becoming more portable every year. It's scary to think that the computing power behind the Apollo unmanned lunar programme was less than that of a pocket calculator. Today, a wristwatch has significantly more power.

However, the rise of the Internet and the exponential growth in data has overtaken our ability to store and run big-data-scale calculations on our desktops. Today's answers to our two challenges of where to store and process data are cloud computing and distributed computing respectively.

Cloud computing

Cloud computing means different things to different people. For some, it's just another way of describing 'IT outsourcing'. Others use the term to refer to any computing service provided over the Internet, and still others define it as any bought-in computer service that sits outside your firewall. Quite simply, with cloud computing, instead of storing all the computer and hardware and software on your desktop or on your company's network, it's provided for you as a service by another company over the Internet in a nebulous 'cloud'.

The goal of cloud computing is to deliver managed services on a pay-as-you-go or subscription basis, saving resources and cost. Typically, you buy cloud computing the same way you'd buy electricity, telephone services or Internet access from a utility company – you can buy as much or as little cloud computing as you need from one day to the next. That's great if your needs are unpredictable: you don't have to buy your own gigantic computer system and have it sit there doing nothing when you're not using it. You don't have worry about buying umpteen licences for processing software and keeping them up to date. You also don't need to worry about viruses infecting your computer, or about backing up the files you create.

The cloud allows you to store and process large amounts of data cost effectively, so you can simply concentrate on your job and leave the problem of providing dependable computing to someone else.

In general, there are three different kinds of cloud computing:

1. **Infrastructure as a service (IaaS):** access to raw computing hardware over the Internet, such as servers or storage. Since you buy what you need and pay as you go, this is often referred to as utility computing.

2. **Software as a service (SaaS):** applications running on someone else's system. Various analytics

packages such as Google Analytics, Kissmetrics and Mix Panel are well-known SaaS providers offering a variety of analytical applications online.

3. **Platform as a service (PaaS)**: provision of a facility to develop applications using web-based tools, running on systems software and hardware provided by another company. You might develop your own e-commerce website but have the whole thing, including the shopping cart, checkout and payment mechanism, running on a merchant's server. WordPress, App Cloud and the Google App engine are examples of PaaS.

Distributed computing

Processing today's large amount of data presents the same challenges that we see with storing the data – traditional methods cannot cope. Calculations over a large amount of data on a desktop could take days or even longer, depending on the volume of data. One solution is to reduce the amount of data used in the calculation. However, more data increases the effectiveness and efficiency of most algorithms, making this approach inadvisable.

Instead, we need to find smarter solutions, such as harnessing the power of multiple computers. This, in its simplest sense, is distributed computing.

A distributed system consists of two or more self-directed computers that communicate through a network to attain a common goal by making use of each computer's local memory. The computers can be used jointly to solve a single large problem by breaking it down into several tasks, with each individual computer tackling a portion of the work on its own.

To the average user, distributed computing systems appear as a single system. However, internally distributed systems are connected to several nodes, each performing its own designated computing tasks. Let's consider the Google web server from users' point of view.

When users submit a search query, they log in to Google.com and search for the required term, apparently making use of a single system. Behind the scenes, though, several systems are working together to complete the task. Google has several servers distributed in different geographical locations that provide the search result in seconds or even milliseconds. This is distributed computing technology.

The advantage is clear: distributed computing systems have more computational power than a centralised computer or even a centralised mainframe. In addition, they allow for incremental growth, allowing organisations to add software and computation power as needed. In turn, this provides a better price/performance ratio than a centralised computer, because adding microprocessors is more economical than buying mainframes. However, rather than purchasing a range of computers to create a distributed network to run calculations, many organisations instead choose to take advantage of the cloud and all that it offers, making it the 'go-to' storage and processing platform for data today.

These days, you can store large amounts of data on cloud-based infrastructure. You can run a range of calculations on that data using a SaaS program, and you can build your own products, such as a tool for marketers to access data about their customers, using a PaaS.

PROCESSING PROCEDURES

Now that we have a strong understanding of data and where it's stored and processed, let's turn our attention to the actual processes that you can put data through. We need to understand what analysis, data science and AI are and how they differ.

However, to understand a process, it's important to first understand its purpose, or the final 'use case' for the raw material undergoing the process. Understanding the use case will help determine what process to put the raw material through.

Consider the diamond-mining industry. Diamonds are most commonly known for their use in jewellery because of their beauty and lustre. However, most diamonds are used in industry. Since diamond is one of the hardest substances known to humanity, many drills or cutting blades have small diamonds on their tips and edges. Diamonds are also resistant to chemicals and able to conduct heat, which is why they are also used to make the infrared windows of fighter planes scratch-proof; in heat sinks, because of their heat-conducting properties; and in X-ray machines. For each of these use cases, the processes that diamonds go through are completely different. The same can be said for data.

So, what is data's use case? There may be many different outcomes for data, but in its simplest form data's ultimate use case is to produce information that informs decision making.

Let's consider a few examples. Facebook has a famous algorithm that it uses on its newsfeed called 'edge rank'. The purpose of the algorithm is to decide which stories appear in each user's newsfeed. The algorithm suppresses what it has termed 'boring' stories, so if your story doesn't have a particular edge rank, few people will see it.

If we consider Amazon's recommendation engine, we see the decision process from two angles. One angle is that it helps Amazon decide which products to push-market to each customer to maximise their basket size in that visit. The other angle is that it provides useful information to the shopper about additional products they might be interested in that are typically bought with their selection.

In life, we take in data every day as information we use for every decision we make. If you consider the organisations that have been successful with data use, this has been a key aspect of their understanding of what data, and in particular big data, is used for.

At Google, for example, senior research scientist Daniel Gillick sees the 'big' in big data as referring to immense changes in how people make decisions: '"Big data" represents a cultural shift in which more and more decisions are made by algorithms with transparent logic, operating on documented, immutable evidence.' Considering that, the key question this section addresses is how the processes of analytics, data science and AI differ if they are all about decision making.

These distinctions are important for every manager or leader to understand, because we now live in a data-driven world where these processes are changing everything. These processes essentially put the science of numbers, data and analytical discovery to work, producing insights and answers to questions that we never thought to ask, fundamentally changing our decisions.

Analytics

The process of data analytics is the application of computational, research and mathematical techniques in the discovery, interpretation and communication of meaningful patterns in data. These patterns form valuable insights that inform decision making, and can be used to uncover correlations and patterns, reducing the need to rely on guesses or intuition.

Florence Nightingale provides an early example of analysis for key decisions by recording and analysing mortality data in her campaigns for hospital and sanitary reform in the 1850s. Nightingale wanted to know the role that hygiene and nursing care played in mortality rates. As a pioneer of analysis, she knew instinct alone would not help her change policy, but analysis of cold, hard data could uncover correlations and patterns that could not be refuted.

Analysis can help provide greater insight into:

- What's happening in a situation
- Why it's happening
- What's likely to happen in the future
- What should be done

What's happening

Although we used analytics way before the recent arrival of big data, the work of applying big data and data science to this type of analysis has become more complex, and the more data we have, the greater insight we can get on what is taking place. With big data, we can monitor a situation as it develops, gathering real-time data and interpreting it immediately, enabling us to react sooner, or decide where to focus our attention. Take, for example, a company that sells electronic devices. On their monthly report they saw a major decline at the end of the month in the number of PCs they had sold, but no corresponding downturn in the sale of any other items. By examining the data in real time it became apparent that the sharp decline was only noticeable for sales after 5pm. Big data yielded a rapid insight into what was happening, and with a level of detail that narrowed the scope of the investigation.

With this data, you can build models that closely resemble the real world, and in this competitive business era, the closer the model is to reality – right now, in your market – the better the chance you have of responding to it before your competition does.

Why it happened

Knowing what happened is good but understanding the reasons why it happened is even better. Big data gives us insight through an enhanced picture of the root cause, exposing unexpected relationships. Following up the previous example on PC sales decreasing particularly after 5pm, a big-data approach would use additional data sources, such as traffic and ordinance data, to identify that for several days that month, the key access road to parking was obstructed by scheduled roadworks after 5pm, suggesting that potential PC buyers arriving with their vehicles after working hours had not been able to get access to parking.

With huge amounts of data from many different data points, the relationships between different variables can be identified and examined in significantly more detail than ever before. This has proven advantageous in many circumstances. Organisations have found that tweaking a certain variable had unexpected consequences or outcomes – good and bad. This 'why it happened' analysis, when merged with 'what happened' analysis, helps make it possible to predict more accurately what might happen next.

What's likely to happen

A key outcome from big data involves running simulations to predict what might happen next. Predictive analytics does not tell us what *will* happen in the future, because no analytics can do that – it's not a crystal ball. However, by studying historical data and identifying insights, trends and patterns we can come up with information about the *probability* of something happening.

The more the data you have, the more accurate the probability of success for your model is likely to be. In addition, the more variations of data you have the easier it will be to identify the range of factors influencing the variable you are trying to predict. By identifying and layering them into your machine-learning models, a more complete picture of the possible future outcome will emerge.

What should be done

Finally, many who are succeeding in cracking the data code are using perhaps the most advanced form of analytics: prescriptive analytics. We'll cover this in more detail later in this chapter, but this exciting practice is helping organisations determine the best course of action for a given situation – and in some cases those actions are programmed to run automatically, without the need for human intervention. Exciting stuff!

Data science

Data science is essentially a more advanced form of analytics, typically used for decisions suitable for automation. As a result, it requires more varied techniques than analytics, to deal with automated movement, analysis and presentation of data. Inevitably, this means that data science is more technical and more expensive than analytics, requiring everything used in analytics and more, specifically in relation to software engineering and technical ability to work with, and manipulate, large amounts of data in a production-ready automated algorithm.

Not every decision can be automated and improved using data science. Therefore, it's important to be sure that the decisions to be made using data science have the right characteristics. Suitable decisions need to:

- be repeatable
- be complex
- have a measurable business impact

Repeatable

When data science solutions are built for decisions that aren't repeatable, you invite redundancy, which is inefficient. There's no value in using an expensive data science process for unrepeatable decisions. Organisations can test the repeatability of a decision by asking themselves these questions:

1. When will the decision need to be made?

2. After the decision is made, is the same type of information considered or analysed again?

3. Are the possible actions consistent from one decision to the next?

4. Can the outcomes of the decisions be measured consistently in terms of business outcomes?

Take, for example, Amazon's recommendation engine, which presents additional items to the user after they've added an item to their basket. Putting this practice through the questions above, we get:

1. Yes, the decision is made every time someone adds an item to their basket

2. Yes, the customer's history, current purchase and other users' previous orders are analysed to identify the additional items to offer

3. Yes, the offers are always products from the existing catalogue

4. Yes, success can easily be defined as a business outcome in increased basket size and sales

It's important to note that decisions, like all things, can change over time. The framework for assessing the repeatability of the decision does not mean that the proposed actions for a decision cannot vary. It's entirely possible for new actions to be defined and old ones retired over time as opportunities for refinement arise.

Complex

This second characteristic of suitable decisions is often misunderstood. For example, many disagree strongly about whether cross-selling is complex, and this is, frankly, where you are most likely to come up against human arrogance.

What can appear to be a simple decision may obscure a deceptively high degree of complexity. For example, consider a charity that must decide what image to add to their new marketing campaign to maximise the total donations that they receive. Some may say that if the charity works with children, any image of a child will do. But should the sentiment be positive or negative? Will the gender or race of the child affect donations? These are complex decisions – ones that require a large amount of experience in any given domain, experimentation and an acute awareness of social nuance to be sure of making the right call.

It's important to recognise that since the data science process represents a significant investment of time and money, organisations will only see a return on investment (ROI) if the decision in question has a high degree of complexity that could not be analysed more cost effectively.

Typically, these are good 'rule of thumb' drivers of complex decisions:

- Policies and regulations

- The requirement for domain knowledge

- The need to analyse large quantities of variables

- The need to select from many possible outcomes

However, unlike repeatable decisions, complex ones do not need to contain all the above drivers. Any one of these drivers may be enough to correctly classify a decision as complex. Also, if the decision only has marginally more than one of the criteria – for example, if it only requires domain knowledge, and a few variables and a few outcomes are to be considered – it too can be considered complex, because of the combination of factors.

Measurable business impact

Since the data science process has a relatively high cost, it's essential to take time to understand the potential ROI before employing it. Both repeatable and complex decisions are likely to show a return since they will be repeated frequently in the future. For complex decisions, poorly defined decision-making approaches are likely to result in poor-quality outcomes. Therefore, the impact of introducing the data science process should be relatively clear.

However, simply being complex or repeatable is not enough. A decision must have a definable, measurable business impact. The cost of poor decisions and the value of good ones should be visible.

Artificial intelligence

AI is probably the most overused buzzword of the age. Mentioning the term 'AI' will likely perk up the ears of an investor, reporter or potential employee. Its profile has soared not only because of its popularity in science fiction movies, but also because of advances in computer power, large amounts of data, new techniques , various public successes and, of course, renewed funding.

AI itself is not new. It was founded as an academic discipline in 1956 on the claim that human intelligence (also referred to as 'natural intelligence') could be taught to a machine, which could then simulate it. The traditional goals of AI included building a machine that could achieve reasoning, knowledge representation, learning, natural language processing, perception and the ability to move and manipulate objects.

To expand on this, the easiest way to think about AI is to consider it in the context of simulating human behaviour. Humans communicate through language by listening and speaking; in the AI world, this requires a machine with speech recognition. We can also write and read text in a language; in AI, this is the field of natural language processing. We can analyse inputs; this is computer processing. We recognise the scene around us through our eyes and organise our images of that world; this is the field of image recognition. We can understand our environment and move around fluidly; this is the field of robotics. We can see patterns and group similar objects; this is the field of pattern recognition.

The human brain is a network of neurons that we use to learn things or remember past events. As the process of AI develops, techniques are being employed to replicate this network and simulate cognitive abilities in machines. This is the burgeoning field of 'neural networks', and as it becomes more deeply complex it will allow us to learn increasingly complex things, referred to as 'deep learning'.

Today, though, the overuse of AI has led to disputes about its scope. One of the key culprits for this is a lack of understanding of machine learning as a technique. When one understands that machine learning *is* a technique, then the natural separation between the processes of analytics, automating decision making (data science) and simulating human intelligence (AI) becomes clear, since each of these processes can use machine learning as a technique for its own specific goal.

SPECIFIC TECHNIQUES

So far, we've talked about the three processes of analytics, data science and AI – but what are the techniques used to actually enact these processes?

The key techniques we must fully understand are statistics and machine learning. All three processes we've covered can use these two techniques with amazing results. Let's consider each of them in detail.

Statistics

Statistics is a branch of mathematics dealing with the collection, analysis, interpretation, presentation and organisation of data. Statistics features heavily in all processes with data, whether you're dealing with analytics, data science or AI. There are four main statistical methods used in data analysis: descriptive statistics, inferential statistics, prescriptive analytics and hypothesis testing.

Descriptive statistics

Descriptive statistics is the most basic branch of statistics. It's used to build models with the objective of analysing historical trends and identifying relevant patterns to gain insights on the underlying behaviour of the data subjects (called the 'population' in statistical language). Typically used when trying to understand the 'What has happened?' question, descriptive statistics is the least complex form of statistics, and is the most commonly used form of analytics for day-to-day functioning.

Inferential statistics

Inferences on mathematical statistics are based heavily on probability theory, which deals with statistical models used to determine the probability of a situation occurring or a future outcome of a decision. This also includes statistical testing, an important function of many digital companies often referred to as 'hypothesis testing' (discussed further below); it is used to predict the likelihood of an event or a result based on a comparison between two or more populations. Using the framework discussed earlier, inferential statistics (also known as 'predictive analytics') help find answers to what could happen.

Inferential models based on inferential statistics enable decision makers to take informed decisions by providing a comprehensive account of the likelihood of an event in the future.

Prescriptive analytics

Prescriptive analytics is the most sophisticated type of analytics, using optimisation and simulation to explore a set of possible options and recommend the best action for a given situation. It involves finding answers to the 'What should be done?' question in a predicted future. It does this not only by showing options and comparing the likely outcomes of actions, but also giving an indication of the effect of future actions on key business metrics and identifying the best actions to drive business objectives. These models are typically the most complex in nature. However, when implemented correctly, they can have a strong impact on a company's decision-making effectiveness and bottom line.

Hypothesis testing

This is a standard statistical procedure that involves testing the relationship between two statistical data sets, or a data set and synthetic data drawn from an idealised model. A hypothesis is proposed for the statistical relationship between the two data sets and is compared as an alternative to an idealised null hypothesis of no relationship between two data sets. Rejecting or disproving the null hypothesis is done using statistical tests that quantify the sense in which the null can be proven false, given the data that are used in the test.

Machine learning

Machine learning is a set of techniques that can provide a computer with the ability to learn without explicit programming. The general idea is that, instead of instructing a computer in what to do, we throw data at the problem and tell the computer to figure it out itself. This is different from programming 'rules'. Tom Mitchell, an American computer scientist known for his contributions in the advancement of machine learning and AI, has provided a comprehensive definition for what machine learning is: 'A computer program is said to learn from experience E with respect to some class of tasks T and performance measure P, if its performance at tasks in T, as measured by P, improves with experience E.'

To put that another way, if a computer program can improve how it carries out or performs a task using its previous experience of understanding what worked or what didn't work, then you can say it has learned. This is quite different from a program that can perform a task because all the parameters and data needed to perform the task have already been defined.

The term 'machine learning' was first coined in 1959 by Arthur Samuel, one of the leading pioneers in the field of AI, best known for his ground-breaking work in computer checkers (draughts), which illustrates what machine learning is. He wrote a program to allow him to play checkers (draughts) against the computer, only teaching the computer (through programming) the rules of legal moves in the game. Every time he played, he won. The computer didn't appear to learn, so he wrote a scoring function that scored the probability that a given board configuration would lead to a winning board vs a losing board after every move. It considered such things as the number of pieces on each side, the number of kings, and the proximity of pieces to being 'kinged'. He also designed various mechanisms for which this computer could become better, allowing it to play itself several times over, to collect more data (or gain more experience) to effectively learn and increase the accuracy of its predictions.

Teaching a computer a simple set of legal rules combined with an ability to understand what a winning scenario could look like caused the computer to suddenly become harder to beat. Arthur Samuel created a machine that surpassed his own ability in a task that he taught it, improving how it performed the task using its previous experience and achieving enough skill to challenge a respectable amateur. This is machine learning.

Machine learning can be separated into three broad categories: 'supervised', 'unsupervised' and 'reinforcement'.

1. **Supervised learning** is when the computer is presented with example inputs and their desired outputs or outcomes, given by a 'teacher', with the goal of learning about the attributes' conditions that maps inputs to outputs. Once the machine is trained, it's given new, previously

unseen data, and the algorithm will use past experience to understand what the result should be.

2. **Unsupervised learning** is when no labels are given to the learning algorithm, leaving the computer on its own to find structure in its input. The computer is never told what the data represents. With enough data, the computer can find patterns in the structures of the data. I like to use the example of listening to hundreds of hours of radio in a foreign language. Your brain will start to form patterns and you'll begin to expect certain sounds at certain times from the patterns that you have heard. If you then watched a movie with visual clues in the same language, your brain would effectively label the data and you will be able to learn the language significantly quicker. This is the key to unsupervised learning. Once the unlabelled data has been processed, it doesn't take many instances of labelled data to understand what is going on. As a representation of today's world, we have a lot of unlabelled data and it's the labelled data that is rarer and more difficult to come across.

3. **Reinforcement learning** is like unsupervised learning in that the data is unlabelled. However, when a computer program interacts with a dynamic environment in which it must perform a certain goal, the outcome is assessed and graded. For example, a computer learns to play a game

and the 'teacher' tells the machine whether it has won or lost. The moves that led to the winning outcome are reinforced as valid moves and, as with unsupervised learning, after many games and constant reinforcement of valid moves for a specific goal, a winning strategy can be created.

PUTTING IT ALL TOGETHER

In today's world, data can be an ephemeral and mis-understood concept. However, looking through the terminologies that we clarified earlier, we can get a better understanding of the three pillars.

1. **What data is** – whether you are talking about big data or just data, they are both simply recorded factual information in all forms. These facts are not limited to measurements and statistics, nor are they limited to sales and profits; they include images, pictures, sounds, behaviours and much more. Big data refers to the fact that the amount of captured information is growing significantly. The numbers that we use to describe the volume of factual information that we are capturing or the variety of factual information, from images and sounds through to behaviours and feelings, are enormous, huge or, to put it simply, big.

2. **What data can do** – when captured, data goes through a system of processing for a purpose. These processing approaches and their

corresponding techniques all serve to help us exploit the data that has been captured. The general purposes for analysis vary from the purposes for AI but they all boil down to five things that they help you do. They can help build a sophisticated understanding of what happened and why it happened. As we increase our sophistication of techniques, data can make predictions and tell us what is going to happen as well as prescribe what we should do in a particular situation. The final frontier is fully automated decision making, where data can be used to automatically understand what has taken place, understand why, predict what is likely to happen, prescribe a solution and execute the chosen solution automatically.

3. **What data is used for** – cast your mind back to the introduction and there you will see that data generates value for all sorts of businesses across all industries. Success in data is not limited to the large West Coast technology giants. But if you look closely at each instance in which it has been used for success, you may notice something interesting: data only has one use case.

Consider the three giants that we often refer to: Facebook, for example, can refer to its newsfeed algorithm as one of its famous data success stories; Google can refer to page rank that it uses to rank search results; and Amazon could cite its recommendation engine. In each case, data is being used for a decision. At Facebook, the edge rank algorithm helps decide what content to serve – it does this automatically. At Google, the page rank algorithm automatically informs the decision on what content to serve and in what order for the user's specific search term. Finally, at Amazon, its recommendation engine automatically decides which products to push-market to each customer.

As this is important yet often overlooked, I will use a couple more examples to make my point. Leading sports teams predict and prevent the onset of injury, prolonging the life and efficiency of their players; this analysis is used to decide what training regime a player should undergo, how many minutes they should play and how often. The world of health and medicine is using predictive data algorithms to identify the onset of certain conditions such as depression; this analysis is used by practitioners to decide when to proactively intervene with a patient to prevent the occurrence of the condition as opposed to traditional expensive, resource-intensive reactive approaches.

To put it simply, every effective use of data is for a decision and it is not limited to internal decisions. Considering the Amazon example earlier, the recommendation engine is there to support the decision of what to serve but from the customer's perspective it is also there to improve the decisions of what else to buy. Therefore, it is important to understand that the scope of decisions is not limited to internal ones but the entire universe of decisions that impact the strategic objectives of the organisation.

With this level of understanding, key individuals in the organisation are better equipped to join the data conversation and be more effective in getting data to work. With this foundation in place, let's move to the next key in cracking the data code: the data leader.

KEY #2
Your Data Leader

Recently, organisations have wrestled with the question of who owns data. The debate has included questions (and strong opinions) such as:

- Should the data owner sit within the organisation, or sit outside to maintain objectivity?

- How senior should the data owner be?

- What title should the data owner hold?

- How much access to organisational strategy should the data owner have?

- Who should the data owner report to?

- What is the data owner expected to do?

- Are there any other roles we should have in addition to a data leader, such as someone focusing on generating value?

These uncertainties have led to a lack of clarity around how best to define the critical role of 'data leader' within an organisation – and this is the cause of many data puzzle failures.

This chapter addresses each of these concerns by explaining why having a data leader is not only beneficial but also critical. I'll then address exactly what you can expect of this role and, importantly, what characteristics the person should have to succeed in the role.

WHY YOU NEED A DATA LEADER

I'm surprised that in today's data-driven economy some organisations are still asking whether they need a chief data officer or a chief analytics officer (titles often used for the data owner of the organisation). I hear this all the time: 'Does my organisation need someone fully dedicated to the process of generating value from data?'

My unequivocal answer to that question is yes – save for a few exceptions, you absolutely need someone dedicated to working with data if you wish to generate the true game-changing value that it promises.

I can group the many possible reasons for this into three clear categories:

1. Research shows a strong correlation between strong company performance and strong data leadership

2. Companies with strong leaders in this role are beginning to see value

3. Someone needs to co-ordinate all the 'moving parts' to value-driven data, from technical components and teams to business management and cultural challenges

Although many of these organisations truly desire to leverage data for competitive advantage, the lack of exclusive data leadership stands out as one of the key reasons for their failure. The fact is, the dynamic nature of business, the need to stay ahead of the competition and the many disruptions in industry have all forced many organisations to revisit how decisions are made and harness the value of all the data available, separating the signal from noise.

From my work with many leading organisations, I've observed that a dedicated data ownership role is *absolutely necessary* in generating value from the over-abundance of data. The person in this role should inspire, promote and drive all activities required to succeed in cracking the data code.

A poll run by a well-known technology researcher found that 45% of the roughly 3,000 companies it regularly polls have assigned someone to oversee their data strategy, while another 16% plan to do so within a year.[3]

Top performers' reporting revenue growth of more than 10% were more likely to have this role on their organisational charts, showing a correlation between strong data leadership and company performance. Of course, correlation is not causation and, at the time of writing, you won't find the role on the management teams of Uber or Netflix because data has been integral to their strategies since Day One. So, while you may believe that it is possible to get data to work without a dedicated data ownership role, don't you want to have the best odds of success?

Organisations that have succeeded in harnessing the game-changing value of data recognise that data leadership is essential. Russell Glass, head of marketing products at LinkedIn, said it best: 'There is no substitute for a corporate leader who has found religion in data and analytics.' This remains true whether you're a team of three in a start-up or a team of twenty in a large organisation.

Due to the growing recognition of both the value of data and the complexities of the technology,

---

3   http://fortune.com/2015/09/03/cio-cdo-strategy/

companies are realising that strong data capabilities are vital and that their data agendas inevitably need strong leadership. So, while simply having someone in the role doesn't guarantee success (there are more pieces to the puzzle), the results show that, to keep up with the competition, having clear data leadership is integral to success.

Without a passionate and skilled leader, even the best efforts around data with the best DSs will flounder. Strong data teams are enablers for success, but on their own they cannot deliver value. Without strong leadership, it's difficult to establish data maturity or culture. Organisations without strong data leadership fall significantly behind their competition in winning, serving and retaining customers.

If you don't have data competency, you need to build it – fast. That's difficult to do, and simply impossible without strong leadership. As discussed, data is complex and requires co-ordination between tech management and business domain experts.

How this new role is defined varies significantly among organisations, though, raising a range of questions:

- What does your data leader look like?
- What should their title be?
- Who should they report to?

To address these questions, we need to build a picture of what the leader of a data initiative needs to do to increase the chances of success.

WHAT YOUR DATA LEADER SHOULD DO

They are responsible for the overall success of the data initiative. It's their job to excite the organisation, get buy-in, engage leaders in the conversation, identify the right opportunities and then develop the best plan for execution.

Put simply, the data leader exists *to generate value from data efficiently, ethically and legally.* To do this, they need to excite, educate and enable the organisation. This requires them to:

- Gain buy-in from the all members of the organisation

- Develop a strong game plan

- Execute the game plan effectively

- Build and manage a high-performance, skilled and motivated team

- Establish a data-driven culture within the organisation

Achieve buy-in

We know that getting data to work is a good idea, but good ideas can be ignored, shot down or wounded so badly that they produce little gain. A seemingly good idea might get 51% of the relevant heads nodding in approval, but the smallest obstacle can easily derail it. Buy-in is therefore more than agreement, approval or consensus – true buy-in is total commitment of time, money and resources wrapped up with a bit of patience.

Achieving buy-in for a data initiative cannot be limited to a few people in the organisation; all parts of the organisation, from marketing and finance to product and even legal, will be impacted by data. Therefore, recruiting representatives from all areas of your organisation as advocates for this change is critical.

Professor John Kotter of Harvard discusses the importance of gaining others' support to create real institutional change, stating:

'Buy-in is critical to making any large organisational change happen. Unless you win support for your ideas, from people at all levels of your organisation, big ideas never seem to take hold or have the impact you want. Our research has shown that 70% of all organisational change efforts fail, and one reason for this is executives simply don't get enough buy-in, from enough people, for their initiatives and ideas.'

There are several approaches to getting this level of buy-in for data and each one will inevitably require help from the C-suite.

The importance of C-suite buy-in

Hierarchy plays a big part in influencing employees in an organisation. Having the support of the C-suite is crucial to the success of any data project for three main reasons:

1. Getting data to work requires its use by key members of the organisation, from product teams through to marketing and finance. Many of these employees must accept some degree of change to how they do things, and people are often resistant to new ideas that threaten the status quo. The support of C-suite members will help encourage acceptance of change throughout the organisation.

2. Getting data from all areas of an organisation together for effective processing and analysis can be a significant challenge, especially for wide-ranging firms with silos in operations and data. Also, data analysis often competes with other corporate initiatives for attention, funding and access to resources. If data deployments

are to be effective, it's important that everyone involved is convinced of the potential value that a comprehensive data plan offers, from the C-suite on down through the ranks.

3. Some see data as a purely technology project, solidly in the realm of the IT department. Directives requesting data or instructing employees how to use what has been created may be ignored if personnel believe it's not beneficial or part of their responsibility. Close collaboration between business units and technical teams is vital in making the most of investments in data initiatives – and the C-suite is critical to ensuring this collaboration happens.

It's essential that the C-suite emphasises the importance of data initiatives and remains congruent with their statements. High-level executives must foster wider acceptance of changes to the status quo and use of the valuable outputs from data. That's why having a clear voice (or better yet, voices) from the top backing, promoting and supporting the investment in data will be so valuable to the success of the investment in the long term.

How to get it

The process of achieving buy-in at the C-suite level is not easy, nor is it a one-off effort. However, if it's your job to take on this task, here are three steps you can follow to help get top-level officials in your organisation to support a data initiative. (And if you are part of the C-suite at your organisation, here's how you can motivate yourself!)

1. **Educate.** To involve the C-suite effectively in data operations, the data leader must educate them about the benefits, particularly since information on how data can be used to improve a business is scarce. While awareness *is* growing among executives about what data is, how to use it and what it's expected to deliver, a recent survey found that 35% of executives admitted they do not understand how data science applies to their specific operations. If executives do not understand the value of data, they will be wary of allocating resources to this area.

   The C-suite must understand the foundational pillars (discussed in the first key) to success (understanding data) to get everyone on board, making it easier to illustrate what returns they can expect to see on their investment – such as increased sales, better customer retention, better margins, improved productivity, etc.

2. **Excite.** Once the value of data is clearly illustrated, the data leader should work to get key players excited about the potential outcomes that an all-out data initiative could have. Think through examples of what each business unit in your organisation could expect if your plan

is implemented. Communicate those outcomes and help the C-suite visualise those benefits. Will marketing spend less time and resources since they'll reach more highly targeted prospects with the insight gained from data analysis? Tell them! Will the product team spend less time developing 'junk features' through gaining a clearer understanding of users' needs? Show them! Will finance see the bottom line grow? Paint a clear picture of the game-changing results a well-supported data initiative should produce and share it enthusiastically!

3. **Understand competing ideas.** Tides can turn quickly in business, causing opinions to change, focus to splinter and support to waver. Industry reports influence executives and new priorities rear their heads in ever-changing markets. It's essential the data leader is aware of the entire business environment including external factors that might impact the C-suite and navigate the process of buy-in accordingly.

This is why I said earlier that obtaining buy-in is not a one-off effort; it's the data leader's responsibility to keep key players in the organisation focused on the prize even as other initiatives compete for their attention, which may involve repeating steps 1 and 2 above continually to maintain interest in your organisation's data initiative.

If gaining buy-in proves especially difficult, you may need to overlap this step with the next one: developing a comprehensive game plan. It may be easier for executives to believe in the possibility of reaping the benefits of big data if they can visualise how the organisation can get there – presenting a 'do-able' plan could be a deciding factor.

Develop the game plan

The process of generating buy-in will always benefit from supporting evidence as to why investing in data is a good idea. The data game plan is a clear written approach outlining the objectives, activities and processes needed to generate the game-changing value that data promises, ensuring that everyone understands what must be done and in what order.

The data leader is responsible for developing this plan, executing it and communicating progress to the leadership team and those who have invested in data. While the details of an effective game plan are covered more thoroughly in Key #3, this section introduces the concept by highlighting the specifics of your data leader's role in the process and steps they can take to succeed.

Developing a credible game plan consists of four key steps, and the sequence is important:

1. **Clearly articulate organisational strategic objectives.** Data can only be considered valuable or successful if it contributes to the goals and objectives of the organisation.

2. **Describe the current position in relation to data.** This is an honest reflection and early self-awareness exercise capturing which components are already in place, which are missing and which need more work.

3. **Identify and prioritise data use cases.** Using what you know about the organisational strategy, list what data output you need and prioritise the effort to obtain it.

4. **Execute the plan.** With these components in place, what must be done and when to move from the current position to the desired end state become clear.

Let's consider each of these components.

Rearticulate the organisational strategic objectives

All efforts to collect, process and apply science to data must be relevant to organisational goals to avoid producing knowledge, insights or complex algorithms that no one can use. To understand what's relevant, all data activities must be filtered through the lens of the organisational strategy.

Although this should be a straightforward exercise, the reality is that in organisations where it's documented, their strategy is contained in reams of documentation or spread across departments, making it hard to read or understand.

Also, organisations typically defer to traditional strategy frameworks such as the classic Five Forces approach or Blue Ocean strategy. However, as work by Boston Consulting Group's strategy experts Martin Reeves, Knut Haanæs and Janmejaya Sinha shows us, there is no one approach that works for everyone. Instead, you must find the best approach for your context considering an increasingly complex environment. Evidence shows that organisations that successfully match their strategy to their specific environment realise significantly better returns.

Therefore, an organisational strategy requires interpretation and rewriting specifically for the data and data science environment; simply understanding the business strategy isn't enough. The data leader must translate it into language that is clear and actionable for those who are executing it in the data puzzle sense.

This is a non-negotiable prerequisite to embarking on any data initiative. Translating the strategy into data terms determines what team is hired, what data is collected, what algorithms are produced and even which use cases should be prioritised (more on use cases below).

Furthermore, this translation is not a one-off activity. Strategy experts have found that the data leader must keep abreast of shifts in external and environmental conditions. Without understanding ever-changing strategic objectives, data science teams can build complex and interesting algorithms that are irrelevant and add little or no value.

The new, rearticulated strategy produced by the data leader is therefore the 'north star', guiding everyone to keep them on track. The Key #3 section in this book details the approach to strategy articulation.

Understand the current state

One of the most important traits of any leader is self-awareness, and the same goes for organisations. Without an understanding of where you are, how can you determine how to reach your destination? The data leader must accurately assess how well the organisation is set up to generate and extract value from data.

In Key #3, I introduce a model for this that can be used to assess the current state, identify what must be done and reveal where to focus both effort and budget to deliver value from data. It considers each of the ingredients required for a successful data initiative and produces a score indicating how well developed each of those ingredients are and the type of work that must be done for each.

This assessment indicates in which of the following areas the data leader needs to focus attention:

- **Strategy.** Sometimes, strategy isn't disseminated well to either the technical or the business teams, leading to key decisions, captured data and a range of haphazard activities that are all poorly aligned with strategy – a situation in which knowledge, insights and algorithms from data are underutilised.

- **Technical.** There may be a requirement to harvest more data, improve the procedures around data processing, and provide tools to improve access to the information for business users, analysts or DSs. There may also be issues with the composition of the data science team and their corresponding output. All of these sorts of issues fall under the technical banner.

- **Data science output.** There may be a requirement to improve the knowledge, insights or algorithms so that they truly answer what or why queries. In some instances, the assessment could highlight that the problem is in progressing from causal analysis to predictive and prescriptive data outputs, or the output may be impressive but poorly aligned to strategic objectives, making it largely unusable.

- **Behavioural.** Developing a data-driven culture in which most of the employees in the organisation take a goal-first approach, seeking to make more informed decisions rather than acting purely on instinct, is the ideal environment for data to thrive. Teams may need to collaborate more closely with those generating value from data. The changes may also involve working on employee motivation, ability or training to ask the right questions of data and witness the amazing value data can bring.

- **Identify data use cases.** The third stage in the development of a data game plan involves defining and prioritising data use cases. Again, Key #3 covers this in more detail, but essentially this is a leadership challenge since a balance must be struck between what is necessary for quick wins to maintain buy-in and work that interests and motivates existing DSs or attracts new ones.

Good DSs tend to be motivated by the work that they are doing rather than just the amount that they are getting paid, so identifying use cases is a critical component of a successful plan. Equally, well-defined use cases should deliver against the business objectives and must be achievable within a reasonable time frame that considers the current state identified during the initial assessment.

As an example, the current state assessment may have found significant weakness in efforts to collect and store data. Therefore, the use case must consider the journey the team is expected to travel given their current state. This is one of the reasons the sequence of these activities is important.

The selected use case will also require buy-in from the leadership team. With excitement around the potential of data, one challenge could be the need to select which leader's objective to pursue. The decision cannot be driven purely on the expected return.

These and other challenges are covered in more detail in Key #3.

Execute the game plan

Execution will inevitably involve the enterprise-wide collection, governance, storage and accessibility of data followed by the application of machine learning and advanced analytics for key business decisions. What data is missing and must be collected? What algorithms must be developed? What methods and technology will we use? How will we share what we've learned from the data, and with whom? While the data leader will typically recruit a team to address each of these components, he or she is ultimately responsible for the team and the work they do.

In each phase of execution, the data leader should ensure that the work being done is both effective and aligned to the business objectives. The intellectual curiosity of the individuals that you're likely to recruit is typically high, which means that the propensity for distraction or the likelihood of selecting untested technology because it's new and exciting is equally high. Such decisions by the team have a cost and will inevitably impact the expected ROI of the solution.

When outlining the work to be done during the execution phase, the data leader must address specific tasks relating to:

- The data-collection process – think back to the raw materials in the previous chapter

- Data architecture and technology – think back to the storage and processing architecture

- The data science process – think back to the procedures in the process as well as the technique

- Data governance – similar to quality control if we continued the diamond analogy

Data collection

Most organisations produce their own data, from transactions and behaviours of customers to sales and customer relationship activities as well as various tests and experiments. The data leader is responsible for ensuring that this data is captured accurately, remembering the adage that rubbish in produces rubbish out.

Also, when possible, external data sources that enrich the existing data should be considered. Today, there is a large amount of externally sourced data that can add significant value when analysed together with internal data. The data leader must ensure that data sourced externally is captured in a format that enables analysis and can be used for training and building complex algorithms. They must also ensure that the data collected is relevant to a data use case identified in the plan and that the team resists the temptation to collect data just because it's interesting. There is value in starting small and then adding more complexity when necessary.

Data architecture and technology

All sourced data will need to be prepared, stored and integrated to support the data use cases identified in the plan. The data leader will need to work with their team to make decisions on how and where the data will be stored, what types of databases will be most efficient (document databases, traditional relation stores) and whether to use the cloud or proprietary technologies and warehouses.

This work is done with an eye on the technical robustness of the data as well as the accessibility for those who work with the data to transform it into knowledge. Some algorithms can be built or trained using data extracted in batches, while others may require a more real-time-based solution for live models that score results and predict real-time outcomes. Whatever the approach, the architecture will need to support the specific requirement for those producing knowledge for the organisation.

The data leader must also ensure that the right technical and architectural decisions are made for the right reasons and to avoid complexity, which often occurs when exploring new, cutting-edge technologies.

In short, the data leader needs to ensure that the data is well organised, accessible and secure before the team of DSs and analysts begin to work with it.

Data analysis and machine learning

At this stage, the key focus of the data leader is to take responsibility for ROI and the impact of analytics and data science, as well as to support actionable insights and informed decision making. They must also keep a close eye on the anticipated costs of, insights and revenue from these deliverables. This is the stage in which the team delivers on the use cases outlined in the early stages of the plan, and it's here that the leader must be wary of a common trait of DSs developing algorithms: seeking unnecessary perfection with little benefit.

I often encounter DSs waiting for the *perfect* sample data set to build or train an algorithm in the hope that it will significantly improve effectiveness. Others would prefer to use the most sophisticated algorithms when basic ones will do. The data leader must maintain the team's focus on the objectives, and in a competitive environment 'good enough' and 'done' is better than 'perfect'.

Data governance

All data will need to follow a set of defined standards, policies and processes to manage its quality, security, consistency and availability from internal and external sources across the enterprise.

This requirement gained prominence after the 2008 recession, when there was a need for greater transparency and increased regulation around capital planning, forcing financial institutions to invest in their data infrastructure and processes for governing data. Since then, there has been an explosion in the amount of data that has been created, and much of it has been personal data which requires stringent regulatory mandates governing its capture, storage and usage. Consequently, all organisations have had to rethink how they govern the data that they collect, store and make available to analysts and DSs to avoid hefty fines and reputational damage. This means that, while the benefits of working with data can be huge, the data leader must keep an eye on any regulatory constraints to truly realise the benefits. For example, they must ensure that information is properly secured, stored, transmitted or destroyed, including security controls that safeguard the integrity and consistency of information that must be stored and archived. It's essential that the leader establishes a consistent version of the truth that the business can trust (for example, calculating the total metric sales in the same way across the business), with ownership for accurate data elements that are supported by a clear enterprise architecture that is legally compliant and secure.

Clearly, there is a lot of work for the data leader to do, but there is more – this is a dedicated role. The data leader needs to take responsibility for all aspects of data, from securing leadership team buy-in to developing and executing against a clear strategic plan.

To succeed, however, planning is not enough. The leader also needs an effective team; none of this can happen without the resource of skilled and motivated people.

Build and motivate a team

The data leader must hire the right individuals to ensure that the data game plan and processes are executed cost effectively and efficiently.

Although I've talked about how big and complicated data is, this doesn't necessarily mean you need a big team, but you will struggle if you only go in search of the one, magical 'unicorn' DS that many believe will solve the puzzle for them single-handedly.

When we think of data, we tend to picture DSs working with statistics and machine learning but, to get data to work for your organisation, you'll need more than just those skills; data needs multidisciplinary teams comprising diverse skills and knowledge. These roles are described fully in Key #4.

The data leader must take time to understand these roles, the talent required for them, look for the resources, train and develop them and, essentially, facilitate delivery of value to the organisation.

Understand talent gaps

The data leader should focus on the talent required and divide it into manageable components based on the initial assessment of the status quo and the suggested use cases that data is expected to deliver.

(Again, this is why the order sequence of these steps is important.)

Some organisations seek to hire for all the needed skills at once. But the data leader should first focus efforts on what's needed to start the data initiative. More resources can be added once the organisation begins to realise value from its efforts.

Find resources

A common misconception is that the skills required to deliver value from data lie exclusively with what the market commonly refers to as DSs. This misconception causes most data leaders to look externally for this role; a more prudent approach would be to begin the search internally.

One of the key benefits of looking internally first is that your existing resources already know the business, and domain knowledge is a critical prerequisite for any successful data initiative. You may already have people who possess data-crunching capabilities and can make data-driven decisions. They might not come from the department you suspected, and they might not sport a badge that reads 'data scientist', but they may have the required skills and already work in your organisation.

If the data leader cannot find the resources internally, then they must conduct a campaign to find the right resources in the marketplace. This is a tricky manoeuvre, and a complete understanding of the qualifications and qualities for each role is required.

Train and develop

Once the team is in position, the data leader must ensure that the team is properly trained and cross-trained. I cannot overemphasise the requirement for domain knowledge and buy-in, and training plays a significant role in this.

DSs and those working on data must have an appreciation for the data's use and the areas where it can generate value, and business users must have some understanding of the data analysis process and its constraints, issues and considerations. Working on data is complex and this can make it difficult for some to understand why certain things are possible or not, why they take a while and what represents a good or impressive result. Cross-training will enhance domain knowledge and buy-in across the teams and remove the destructive 'us vs them' culture that can easily develop.

The data leader's goal is to establish a common language that the group can use to collaborate effectively and share a vested interest in the success of the outcome. This mutual understanding will increase effectiveness when these two groups work together on your initiative.

Motivate the data team

Due to the scarcity of data-savvy resources in today's market, data teams tend to be expensive. However, it's generally not money that motivates these individuals. Because they typically enjoy working on groundbreaking solutions for business problems with the latest technologies, the best individuals are actually more motivated by their work. Interesting projects are therefore key to attracting and motivating DSs.

This creates both an opportunity and a challenge for the data leader. On one hand, they need to provide interesting problems with the freedom to explore and solve them using exciting techniques. On the other hand, these ventures come at a cost, and the data leader must find a balance between finding solutions quickly and effectively while pushing the boundaries of technology when appropriate.

The best way of striking this balance is to minimise the number of use cases to focus on and develop an agile approach, ie, deliver a 'version one' that works and begins to deliver a return, and then iterate on the sophistication of the solution for a more fine-tuned result.

Establish a data-driven culture

Algorithms can work effectively in a test environment, but they must be deployed and used in the real environment to generate a return. Typically, the areas in which these models can be deployed or used are outside of the technical team – either in product development, marketing, finance or operations, who may not be motivated to adopt them. To help increase the chances of usage, the data leader must seek to establish a data-driven culture throughout the entire organisation.

Becoming a data-driven company is about more than just collecting data and looking at it occasionally. To be truly data driven, businesses need to make the transition from gut-based decisions to an approach that seeks to make every decision more informed by relevant data, enabling the data to reveal conclusions that drive the direction of the company.

In a data-driven organisation, all employees are expected to collect, understand and learn from data on a regular basis, essentially reaching fact-based conclusions that can be supported with metrics. Data should be shared and used for planning and reporting purposes along with internal monitoring against goals and objectives.

Being a data-driven organisation results in more reliable decisions, informs effective practices and enables awareness of issues, innovations and even solutions. It also accelerates consensus, which decreases the likelihood of algorithms and other technological efforts being left unused.

Creating a data-driven culture is not easy. Shifting the corporate culture from an intuitive, gut-based approach to a more objective, data-driven one requires a change in behaviour throughout the organisation, starting with the most influential people. To accomplish this, the data leader must create structures and conditions that motivate employees to develop a data-driven mindset and provide timely triggers about the data available and how it can be used for the key decisions they need to make.

The data leader must create a structure where employees understand the value of being data driven and are incentivised to use this approach. Leaders should be led to see value in making decisions based on data justification as opposed to accepting the most popular or loudly postulated opinions.

Another key to establishing a data-driven culture is to ensure that decision makers have easy access to relevant data and that it's presented in a way that makes sense, otherwise it won't be used. 'I can't access the data and I need to make this decision now, so we'll just make this call based on what I believe' is a common excuse when data is complex and difficult to access. If people can access the information they want in the way they want it, when they need it, the level of trust in data will grow exponentially.

Establishing this motivational framework requires the support of the senior leadership team, and this says quite a lot about the required seniority of the data leader. Imagine trying to effect this degree of widespread cultural change from a low rung on the corporate ladder!

ABOUT THE DATA LEADER

With a clear understanding of what is expected of the data leader, we can now consider who this person is. How can data science become a core and strategic component of an organisation if no one at senior level takes responsibility for it? Without someone to steer the ship and oversee all the activities described above, how does the organisation maximise the value it gets from data and data science?

This section considers how senior the position should be within the organisation, the position's title, who the data leader should report to and how to hire the perfect candidate.

Who is the data leader?

Simply by acknowledging the data leader's brief, it's clear that this person should be a senior-level candidate. The requirement to work across the organisation, influence changes in behaviour among all employees and have a firm grip on organisational strategy indicate that the data leader should be a member of the C-suite.

Because of the obvious relationship between data and technology, many organisations allocate the role of delivering value from data to the CIO. Others choose the CFO because of their number-crunching skills or select the CMO based on marketing's focus on understanding customers. Sadly, many of these organisations fail to win at the data puzzle game since using a member of the existing C-suite usually results in data silos. Where data and data science operate in silos, benefits from interdepartmental data cannot be realised. The process of maximising value from data science requires data that spans all business units, databases and reporting hierarchies.

In addition, the individuals in existing C-suite roles are entrenched in their own areas of expertise and typically have difficulty developing the 'big-picture' mentality needed to get true value from a cross-organisational data initiative. Moreover, they can't effectively focus on their current responsibilities and simultaneously strategise and carry out all that is required to generate value from data – that is, run a comprehensive change programme that develops a data-driven culture and ensure that the analysis and data products created are used by all the relevant teams for the overall benefit of the organisation.

Without a dedicated resource to navigate complex contemporary organisations, it's difficult to focus on ensuring that high-quality value is being created from data. The responsibility for the success of data science cannot be part of someone's role; it requires dedicated focus at a senior level.

Following rising awareness of this fact, two new roles are fast emerging at the C-suite level, signalling that data and generating value from it is a high priority in business today: the chief data officer (CDO) and chief analytics officer (CAO).

CDO or CAO?

In business, the word 'chief' in a title is a relatively new addition. A study from University of Michigan found that, in 1955, the title CEO (chief executive officer) was only found in one out of 200 of the largest industrial firms in the United States. Fast forward to 1975 and almost all of those 200 firms had adopted the title. A similar trend was found with the title CFO: in 1964, none of the 400 largest organisations had the title but, by the year 2000, more than 80% of them did.

In fact, most companies over the last twenty years have added new C-level roles in response to changing business conditions. We have the CIO and the CTO (chief technology officer), who became prominent with the rise of information technology, programming and software development in business processes. The chief strategy officer joined to address an increasingly complex and rapidly changing global market, and the CMO became essential when new channels and media raised the complexity of brand building and customer engagement.

Today, the business environment is going through some seismic changes. Organisations seeking to generate value from data must understand how to tame the rapidly increasing quantities of data being created, identify talent to manipulate it and invest in the new technical infrastructure required to exploit it. These objectives will enable an organisation to use data to implement new features, identify optimisation or performance opportunities and generate incremental revenues. Hence, many organisations have concluded that there is a requirement for extra executive muscle to meet these new conditions, and so the CDO and CAO roles have been created.

Often, these roles are used interchangeably, but there are differences. In short, the CDO deals with the collection, storage and processing of data, while the CAO focuses on building insights on the data prepared by the CDO. Both roles are essential, but adding them both to the C-suite can overcrowd the executive team and stretch resource budgets. Depending on the size of the organisation and the complexity of the data, it's possible for one role to do both – but it does take a rare combination of skills to effectively manage both sides of the equation.

The bottom line is titles are not terribly important in this decision. The key point to remember is that regardless of who is selected or what title, the data leader must extend their responsibilities to capture all the requirements covered earlier. Whether this person is called a CDO or a CAO, once in the C-suite they are responsible for generating value from data efficiently, ethically and legally.

Who should the data leader report to?

I attended a round-table discussion on data and was fortunate to be surrounded by most members of the C-suite. During the discussion I captured the most prominent thoughts from each executive on the topic of data.

CIO: How do I...

- build and deliver the information systems to support this data?

- ensure that the data we collect is legally compliant?

CTO: How do I...

- apply our standard development methodologies and technical policies to the data platform, access layers and APIs for the analysts?

- ensure that the code that harvests data for data science is in line with our IT development standards?

CFO: How...

- much is all of this going to cost?

CMO: How do I...

- use this output from data to increase the value that I can generate from customers?

- use this when we communicate with customers, for example through targeted customer relationship management (CRM) communications?

- use this for targeted acquisition, retention, ads and commercials?

CPO (chief product officer): How do I...

- use this to define the products that I should be building?

- use this to build smarter products?

CEO: How do I...

- use this to run my business effectively?

Each executive had their own perspective which related to their own area when it came to data, but only the CEO seemed to hone in on understanding how it could be used across the entire organisation – and this is typical; it's the CEO who has the oversight to consider all areas of operation.

Therefore, the data leader should only report to the CEO or chief operating officer (COO) to signal to everyone that data analytics is an important, valuable and strategic initiative in which the organisation believes and is banking on to realise value. The simple truth is that in business seniority and reporting line signal business priorities. Transforming organisations to move from their traditional work approach to a more data-first approach is a major shift of behaviour, that requiring strong, visible support of key individuals like the CEO or COO. Therefore, if your company truly wants to unlock the value from data it must signal to the business that data is indeed a priority.

Characteristics of the data leader

With such a wide brief, you might think you're looking for a mythical unicorn. It's rare to find an individual with the wide spectrum of skills required to succeed as a data leader.

The data leader must have the technical ability to understand the complex algorithms produced through data science. (Although they don't have to know how to build them – that's what the team is for – they must understand enough to know what's needed for each use case and business need.) They must be well versed in the world of data regulations and governance requirements as well as the technical architectures, languages and best practices needed to deliver complex analytics solutions. They must understand data-collection methodologies, the basics of logical architectures, analytical methods and the basics of machine learning. Speaking the same language as the data team is mandatory.

In addition to these technical abilities, they should have experience operating at a senior leadership level, ie, be able to communicate with individuals at all levels, influence and generate buy-in for new ideas and concepts and deliver organisational behavioural change.

They must also be business savvy, with a strong commercial sense and the ability to tell an exciting story about data. They must have well-honed leadership skills that inspire trust and respect. Finally, they must be focused on understanding the process of managing people, motivating them and keeping them interested in the work to be done.

In my experience, all organisations that have succeeded in extracting value from data have a data leader possessing the skills and characteristics described here.

Once you appoint a qualified and experienced data leader to spearhead your data initiative, it's time to begin the monumental task of creating your data game plan.

KEY #3
A Game Plan For Big Data

As with most efforts in business, to successfully implement a big-data solution you'll need a big-data game plan. This game plan is a strategy that identifies what big data is going to achieve for your organisation and the path that must be taken to do so.

There are three major steps in developing your big-data game plan:

Step 1: Clarify the business strategy. Achieve and document an understanding of what the organisation is trying to accomplish from a strategic perspective. You must have a clear understanding of the goals, objectives and any scope constraints of the strategy. It's important to note that the focus of this step is not to develop a *new* business strategy, but instead to develop a succinct and clear understanding of the *existing* strategy.

Step 2: Define and prioritise data use cases. This step relies heavily on the previous step, using the corporate strategy to produce a prioritised list of use cases for data that directly align with and deliver against the strategic objectives of the organisation. Keep in mind that the big-data use cases may involve selling data if the organisation produces information that is valuable to outsiders but is within the value chain of the respective industry.

Step 3: Create a plan for execution. Outline the activities required to deliver solutions to the identified use cases. To do this, you first need to understand the current state of the organisation in relation to its ability to deliver data solutions. This step begins with a capability assessment, a process of building an understanding of how well the organisation is set up to generate value from data. This will present a clear view of your strengths and weakness with respect to big data, identifying which areas need more work or additional focus. Understanding current capabilities allows you to outline the activities required to deliver the desired use cases.

By delivering these use cases efficiently, the organisation will realise the desired impact on the goals and objectives of the organisation.

CLARIFY YOUR BUSINESS STRATEGY

A well-articulated and clearly understood strategy helps make key decisions in an organisation. Whether the decisions relate to hiring and firing, resource allocation and prioritisation or any other operational issue, the strategy is the guiding light that sets the boundaries and direction. For most tasks in an organisation, a clear strategy will increase focus and ensure that the investment in effort contributes to the agreed direction of the organisation. This holds true for data.

Typically, knowledge from data is generated through a process of data science and machine learning and, as it turns out, machines are most effective at making use of the knowledge that they create when they understand the strategy. To illustrate, let's reconsider the work of Arthur Samuel in his quest to teach a computer how to play checkers (draughts).

Initially, Samuel gave the machine a set of rules to operate under and the computer won on a couple of occasions. However, it wasn't until he provided the machine with an understanding of what an efficient strategy looked like that the machine began to become an effective checkers player, beating him on all occasions. If this works for a machine, then it's an ideal approach for getting data to work.

It might sound like a clichéd first step, but success from big data requires a razor-sharp understanding of what the organisation as a whole is trying to do. This applies to all organisations regardless of size or industry – whether you're a new tech start-up, a small retail outlet or a large established organisation, the first non-negotiable step to establishing value from big data is a comprehensive understanding of the organisational strategy.

For this to work, the assumption is that your organisation already has a strategy. The purpose of this phase is to build a comprehensive understanding of it so that you can start the process of building the data decision inventory (or, use cases). It's an approach that works with an *existing* strategy to extract the key components required for big data and data science. Without the extraction of these key points, teams suffer from a lack of focus and transparency, resulting in a significant increase in the chances of experiencing poor returns from the initial investment.

If your organisation does not have an existing strategy developed, an effort should be made to create one separate from your data initiative – as soon as possible!

A lack of strategy

The absence of a clear strategy (for your organisation in general and for your data initiative) typically translates into a lack of focus on the objectives of the organisation. This can easily lead to efforts spent on collecting data and building algorithms just because they are interesting and *might* prove useful. In turn, this increases costs, consumes valuable time and contributes only slightly if at all towards the objectives of the organisation. This 'drag' will significantly reduce the chances of realising ROI.

Some hold the view that data professionals should be left to explore the data and see what it says. Large organisations like Tesco, Facebook or Amazon collect a huge amount of data because they can. They have large teams that analyse the data and produce valuable knowledge, insights and algorithms. Collecting what you want and exploring with the hope of finding a useful gem costs money, but these companies can afford it. I recently found out that a team at Facebook can predict when your status is going to change from single to married. For the moment, this is an interesting insight that may not immediately be relevant, but they have the resources, skills and luxury of time to act on it if/when they choose.

Generic exploration like this can be useful and can unearth incredibly valuable insights but, in reality, most organisations don't have the budgets or access to a huge talent pool to endlessly mine big data sets in the hope of uncovering them. For those that cannot do this, the lack of focus can result in the organisation sinking in data yet hungry for actionable insight. This puts any expected ROI at risk because big data is only valuable when it is used appropriately to deliver real results. It is necessary to allocate some time for exploration but this shouldn't exceed 10% of the total time spent, with the remaining time being spent focused on the strategic objectives.

Extracting key components of strategy for big data

The purpose of this step is not to rewrite your organisation's strategy, but to extract key elements to make your data strategy snappy and easy to digest, to serve as a north star for all the key decisions. The strategy doesn't have to be written elegantly for data teams to understand it. All that's required is an explicit articulation of a few specific components, presented clearly so that the decisions required to prepare the data strategy are easier to understand and make.

This may seem obvious but, sadly, it is not typical; key components tend to be buried in long and complex strategy documents or, worse, aren't even listed but instead are left to the interpretation of a few members of the leadership team. In short, organisational strategies come in many shapes and sizes, making them difficult to understand and implement.

Consider these statements, which you may have heard before or even made yourself:

- 'I don't know whether we should be pursuing this opportunity. We're getting mixed signals from the top.'

- 'I really think we should be focusing on this initiative, but it's been shut down because apparently it doesn't fit the strategy.'

- 'Why are we doing this? It seems so out of left field.'

Such confusion and frustration are common and in a surprisingly large number of companies, executives and frontline staff alike express frustration at the lack of a clear expression of their strategy. When you have tens, hundreds or thousands of smart people working in an organisation, each making what they believe to be the right decision for the company without the required level of clarity, the net result is confusion and poor overall company performance.

A recent Harvard Business Review found that organisations with a concise, easy-to-understand strategy statement widely understood by everyone (regardless of seniority) experienced better overall business performance – especially when compared to organisations in which the strategy was complex, extremely detailed and not rolling off the tongue of every employee.

Organisations that overcomplicate their strategies typically have leadership teams that fail to appreciate the requisite need for simplicity, clarity and digestibility. As a result, most of these leaders are left mystified when their well-crafted strategy, filled with elegant prose, was never implemented.

One of the key reasons we see this level of confusion is simply due to the plethora of frameworks, methodologies and approaches that have been designed to help produce organisational strategies. These include many familiar tools such as the Ansoff Matrix, Porter's Five Forces, the Three Cs or the Five Ps, the SWOTs, PEST, etc. By my count, since we entered the twenty-first century, we have seen more than fifteen new approaches and frameworks, from Blue Ocean to the Adaptive Advantage approach. Therefore, it's no surprise that most people, including business leaders, are unable to articulate their organisation's strategy – or when they do, it's nearly impossible to find a colleague who would articulate it the same way.

To extract value from data and map the decisions where data science can add value, the strategy statement should be communicated with short, concise and easy-to-understand verbiage that everyone in the organisation, regardless of their role or seniority, can understand and recite. To do this, executives need a clear definition of the key components that should make up a strategic statement. Such clarity will make the process of formation, communication and internal understanding significantly easier, greatly increasing the probability of successful implementation.

Components of the business strategy for data

Three specific components must be evident in your statement of the business strategy for data.

1. **Strategic objective** – a comprehensive definition of the end goal

2. **Scope** – an indication of the limitations or boundaries of operation

3. **Key actions** – an indication of how each department contributes to the overall company objective

Defining these components has important benefits for the process of understanding and making key decisions. In organisations where the strategic objective, scope and key actions are clearly articulated, anyone in the organisation can make decisions that are in line with strategy without the need for regular guidance and micro-management. Take Admiral Horatio Nelson and the Battle of Trafalgar, for example. The British captains had been aware of Admiral Nelson's strategy (dubbed 'Nelson's touch') for three weeks and had such a clear understanding of that strategy that they were trusted to act on their own initiative once battle had commenced – unlike captains of the

Combined fleets (French and Spanish). This clarity enabled the British fleet to win the Battle of Trafalgar.

Let's consider each of these components in more detail to understand what is required to get them right.

Objective

Most companies have what they believe to be a clear strategic objective when they formulate their strategy, but it is usually not a 'well-formed' outcome. Many of these companies confuse their mission and/or vision statement with their strategy statement. This may also be because the many definitions of mission and vision that exist. One thing that is clear is that neither the vision nor the mission statement should contain specific numerical targets. Instead, they should summarise why the company exists and what it broadly aims to achieve. Together they comprise a *high-level* guide and target for the strategic objective. The strategic objectives are therefore small steps that, when achieved within a specific time period, lead the company closer to its target. It is important that the strategic objective for data be a single objective. This is the way algorithms work, so this is the way to make data strategies effective and actionable. The key to a well-formed strategic objective is therefore for it to be specific, measurable, achievable, realistic and time-bound. One approach is to ask yourself the following questions:

- What is the one thing that we need to focus on doing to achieve our mission?

- How will we recognise that we have achieved this?

- When will we realise that we have achieved this?

Some argue that the answers to these questions are obvious and don't need to be written down. However, in today's complex and ever-changing business landscape, it's not safe merely to hope that assumptions are understood and acted on. Leaving out any of these components only increases the risk of failure, so it's a better idea to address them.

Thinking about the objective in the framework of these questions connects strategic thinking and strategic action, moving from pure desires to realistic, achievable objectives – resulting in a higher chance of success. When these conditions are met, the objectives that will drive the organisation over a defined period will be clear, bringing us closer to understanding the key decisions that we need to make to deliver the strategy.

The choice of this objective will inevitably have a profound impact on the organisation and in my experience will always result in passionate and intense debate that eventually forces alignment in the leadership team. Consider an example taken from a *Harvard Business Review* article on strategy in which a profit-maximising company adopted the objective to 'generate at least 10% organic growth per year'.[4] This change forced the firm to shift from serving only its profitable core customers, managing costs and seeking efficiencies, to developing a raft of new products and services appealing to a much wider set of customers.

Scope

Today, most organisations operate across a wide spectrum of activity. Defining the boundaries, constraints and limitations is essential for operating efficiently and preventing investments and effort from being spread too thinly. It's crucial to define the scope, or domain, of the business: the part of the landscape in which the firm will operate.

I did some work for an employee engagement company that needed to make a decision about who their customer was. Taking on projects for both start-ups and large corporates was not a financially viable option since each type of customer had significantly different approaches to running their business. This affected decisions from marketing, sales, hiring and even, to some extent, the office décor. It was therefore vital to understand which customer type their scope would be limited to.

When it comes to understanding where data fits in, scope not only delivers a clear picture of boundaries

---

4   Collis, DJ, and Rukstad, MG, 'Can you say what your business strategy is?', *Harvard Business Review* 86, No. 4 (2008).

to operate within, it also provides a clear articulation of what should *not* be done. Some believe that this can be a constraint on creativity, but that would only be true if the purpose of scope was to tell you exactly what to do. Scope is purely about boundaries and known constraints, indicating where organisations should and should not go; it does not prescribe actions and activities. Instead, a correctly articulated scope limited to an explanation of the boundaries enables experimentation and initiative within a specific domain.

Knowing limitations and boundaries plays a crucial role when it comes to understanding the key decisions that big data will support and enhance.

When defining the scope, these three areas must be considered:

1. The customers, offering or product

2. Location

3. Industry or vertical integration

Depending on the organisation and strategy, each of these dimensions may vary in relevance. For the engagement consultancy mentioned earlier, the scope was around the customer. For organisations with multiple products or those that operate globally, the scope must clarify which products are included or excluded, and in which regions. Let's look at TED as an example: a media organisation that posts talks online for free distribution. TED has a clear mission to spread ideas; we could extrapolate a strategic objective of 'moving from 200,000 users per month to one million users per month in two years.' (Notice the specific, measurable and time-bound strategic objective).

It's vital to clarify the scope, because their users consist of presenters and viewers, both of whom could be new or returning. They have the choice of ignoring the type of user, in which case the scope includes all users, or they could decide that actually they need to achieve that number mainly by growing new viewers. Definitions of scope are needed to inform the next and final part of the business strategy: the actions – each of which defines what everyone across the business has to do to contribute to the strategy.

Key actions

Objective and scope alone are usually not enough. Understanding the key actions of each part of the organisation is a prerequisite for identifying where data can quickly add value or enhance the benefits that it offers to the business

Clarifying the responsibilities of each of the functions reveals the objectives of all decisions made within each department or business unit. I could have called this section understanding business functions, or roles and responsibilities, but, in truth, we must not forget that as data is purely about decisions, the step that follows a decision is an action.

To return to the previous example, where we looked at the online organisation TED, let us assume that the objective of 'moving from 200,000 users per month to one million users per month in two years' has a limited scope targeted at viewers. The statement is then adjusted to read 'moving from 200,000 users per month to one million users per month in two years by focusing on increasing the number of viewers'. The actions section of the business strategy would be as outlined below.

Business area	Action
Product	Build and enhance the product to increase the number of monthly users from 200,000 to one million in two years by focusing on increasing the number of viewers
Marketing	Recruit new users and engage existing viewers to increase the number of monthly users from 200,000 to one million in two years by focusing on increasing the number of viewers
Content	To upload new content that will increase the number of monthly users from 200,000 to one million in two years by focusing on increasing the number of viewers.

From this we can begin to see the use cases that we would to define and quantify under each part of the business.

DEFINE AND PRIORITISE USE CASES

A data use case is an application of the knowledge, insight or automated algorithm gained from data to further an organisation's business goals which are tied to the organisation's well-defined strategy. The key non-negotiable step when launching your data initiative is to identify, describe and model the use case or use cases that will repay the investment in data. This section focuses on the process of identifying and prioritising suitable use cases.

In Key #1, Demystifying Data, I used a few examples to illustrate that data's ultimate use case is to produce information that informs decision making, ie, data is processed to understand what has happened, why it happened and/or when it is likely to happen, to inform or automate a decision. Facebook's edge rank algorithm automatically decides which stories appear in each user's newsfeed, and Amazon's recommendation engine automatically decides which products to push-market to each customer. Based on this, the data use cases represent one or many *decisions* that a company needs to make. All decisions require some form of data in order to be made effectively, but not all decisions are suitable for full algorithmic automation.

The process for identifying and prioritising use cases therefore starts by identifying all of the decisions that drive the organisation and then producing a decision map. This is essentially a document that outlines the key decisions, how they relate to the strategy and what knowledge is required to make the decision. The following list of key decision discovery questions outlines what you are trying to capture in this process.

1. What are the decisions that need to be made?

2. How do they relate to the strategy?

3. What are the micro decisions required?

4. Who owns each one?

5. How often are the decisions made?

6. How many people are involved in the entire decision-making process?

7. How do these decisions relate to one another?

8. How much does each decision cost?

9. How much is the attributed return?

10. What knowledge is needed to make each decision an effective one?

Interestingly, before I launched my business, I had not come across an organisation that had taken this step or even attempted to produce a decision map or even a decision inventory. Without knowing the answers to these questions, how will your organisation find the use cases for your data? How will you decide which use case will have the most impact?

Although you are likely to want to start getting results as soon as possible, it's worth noting that, for a large organisation, attempting to develop an enterprise-level decision map as a single project is not a good idea. There's the inevitable risk that this process will take too long, greatly delaying implementation of any improvements and resulting in no visible return on the time invested. This is a good way to kill any buy-in that's been achieved!

For large organisations, I suggest using the scope component of business strategy clarification to home in on a specific area of the business, or at least on a closely linked set of business processes, essentially identifying a specific strategic business area and producing the decision map for that area.

Discovering the decisions

There are several ways to find, gather and map decisions. They range from high-level, generic, collaborative, workshop-type approaches to more procedural, structured and analytical procedures. In data we use a process known as triangulation, where we ask the same question from three different perspectives to help us verify the output. When identifying decisions, I suggest that you use the same approach, and the following perspectives align neatly with the three recommended discovery approaches to build a decision map:

- Executive discovery

- Operational discovery

- Industry discovery

Each approach will differ, depending on a range of factors, from how many people there are in the organisation, how new or established the business is, to the general leadership styles across the senior teams. In some organisations the leadership only concerns itself with the big decisions. In others the leaders are hands on and insist that every decision must go through them. The nature of the business also has an impact on how decisions are made. Some areas of business, such as consumer credit cards, property and insurance, are more decision-centric by nature and therefore we can expect greater transparency in this process, with more legal checks and balances.

To complete this stage of the strategy successfully, best practice dictates that you use more than one approach to validate the decisions discovered, since each approach is likely to identify a set of decisions that another approach may not have uncovered. The key is to ensure that you include key individuals during your chosen process to get early buy-in and reduce the likelihood that an important use case will be missed.

Executive-level discovery

Of the three approaches examined, this is probably the least analytical, but the one with most valuable political advantages.

This process involves a series of brainstorming workshops with the leadership team, who are effectively the key decision makers in the organisation. The purpose of each session is to list all the key decisions that they believe need to be made on a day-to-day basis to achieve the strategic objectives. You may find that decisions identified using this approach typically don't exhibit the right level of detail, therefore it can be helpful to ask what decisions their *staff* make and how these decisions get escalated, but without getting bogged down in detail, as the other approaches are designed to capture this additional information.

There is a natural tendency to focus on internal decisions, but it's useful to get the executive perspective on external customer or supplier decisions, together with a view on their impact on the strategy, thereby building an understanding of which way these decisions go when customers or suppliers are satisfied or unsatisfied.

Working with the executives during this decision discovery session is an excellent approach to obtaining early buy-in for the data initiative by focusing on things that matter to the senior leadership team. With the leadership team involved at this stage, securing budget and executive-level sponsorship is much easier. Of course, a poorly run workshop could also kill the project before it even starts, so this approach does carry some degree of risk. (Having a seasoned business analyst lead the meeting will help – more on that in Key #4.)

Operational discovery

Similar to the executive discovery, this approach will involve a series of workshops with operational staff. However, during these workshops it is essential to spend time thinking in more detail about the following:

- **What micro decisions are needed to make the higher-level decisions that the executive team outlined?**
  We often find that while the leadership team can identify an important decision that needs to be made to achieve the strategic objective, there are often smaller decisions that have to be made before that. These are called micro decisions and are typically low-level operational decisions that executives, particularly in large organisations, do not typically concern themselves with.

- **What do you need to know to make each of the decisions?** As you deconstruct each decision, you should begin to identify where data and advanced analytics can play a significant role in ensuring the efficiency of that decision by clarifying whether it's purely data that's required for the decision, or an advanced analytics process/algorithm, or a set of structured rules. When it comes to pulling out the respective use cases, this level of detail will play a big part in generating an understanding of what to do.

To do this, take time to document all the knowledge required to make the decision and where that knowledge resides. As a quick example, knowledge about a customer's propensity to purchase an upsold item may be required in deciding whether to send them an upsell product email. This knowledge may be embedded in experience, wisdom, judgement or an algorithm that calculates the probability of purchase. Another example might be an email designed to encourage a customer to complete their profile. In this instance, the knowledge required may only be a list of which users have not completed their profile – this information might be in an internal database in the form of raw data. Other examples may require data from external systems, such as weather data or social connections.

- **How often are these decisions made?** We also need
  to capture frequency, timeliness and consistency
  for each decision. Some decisions only need to be
  taken once a week, while others must be made
  every hour. Some can wait for another decision
  to be made, and others are needed in real time
  or they lose value. Some are constants and
  never change, while others change with every
  adjustment in the environment.

- **What processes will help to achieve the key objectives
  of the team?** Analysing processes found in day-
  to-day operations is a great way to discover key
  decisions. While they are not always obvious
  and are sometimes hidden deeply in the process
  design, many decisions that come out of this
  method are suitable for a big-data algorithm.
  It's important, therefore, to search carefully for
  explicit decision points and any escalation routes
  in each process examined.

  Explicit decisions occur in two circumstances.
  The first is when there's a task followed by
  multiple paths dependent on a decision task,
  usually represented by diamonds in flow charts
  and process maps. Think of it as a fork in the
  road, where a chosen direction could only happen
  because of a decision. The second circumstance is
  during the occurrence of a decision verb: resolve,
  calculate, select, choose, validate, determine, etc.

Typically, explicit decisions are quite clear, but the outcomes could differ in certain circumstances. For example, consider organisations in different regions. The same explicit decision might result in a different outcome depending on which region you are in. Capturing these can reveal additional decisions that must be considered when creating the decision inventory to identify use cases.

Finally, in some processes, the activity must physically stop so you can consult a certain person. This is an *escalation point* and typically happens when additional knowledge is required to make the decision. You sometimes see this in shops with damaged goods being returned, or when a customer asks for a discount and the assistant must get a manager's approval. The individual making this decision needs to apply judgement to make the decision. Even though, typically, these decisions are made by human beings, they make good candidates for big data as they are repeatable.

- **What key events impact the decisions and how do they do so?** Looking at different events is another useful approach to decision discovery. External events such as a major news story, a storm, changes in regulations, increased competition – all these events and more can affect logistics and operational decisions.

In fact, a new piece of legislation may result in
an entire business restructure during which new
decisions must be introduced for the business to
remain a going concern. For example, European
legislation on how an organisation can capture
and store personally identifiable information
has and will continue to have a major impact on
many organisations.

Events can be macro, as described earlier, or
micro, such as when a customer visits my website
and clicks on a button.

- **What metrics are impacted by these decisions?**
  Some decisions can be discovered by looking at
  an organisation's key performance indicators
  (KPIs) or the key metrics that give an indication
  of business performance, and then working
  backward to see which decisions move those
  indicators. Linking as many decisions as possible
  to the metrics is an essential step when it comes
  to identifying which will make powerful data
  use cases because we are not just looking at any
  metric but at those already identified by the
  business as key metrics needed to assess how
  well the organisation is performing.

Industry discovery

Understanding your industry value chain is another
good way to determine the decisions that affect your

organisation, or decisions that your organisation can have an impact on.

You'll find that value from data need not be limited to internal decisions – they can be external, too. Consider JustGiving.com. One of their goals is to grow the world of giving, and in the value chain of their industry, charities make key decisions that can be informed by data that JustGiving.com holds.

For example, charities may need to understand what images are most effective for their campaigns, or who to target with what messaging to increase the chances of a donation. Since JustGiving.com has a large user base along with a repository of images and emails with a range of messages, they're well positioned to be the sole providers of this validated information for other charities.

All information gathered from these discussions and workshops needs to be documented in a way that is easy to understand and manage. Thinking about what needs to be in the document will also ensure that the workshops and discussions capture the right decisions.

Prioritising decisions on use cases

Organisations are likely to have multiple decisions that are use-case candidates for big data, and therefore need to consider which ones to do first. This step in the process requires all stakeholders to work together, including the advanced analytics team, members of the leadership team and any individuals with strong business acumen and a good understanding of the level of cost, difficulty to implement and potential impact on the business of each decision.

The best way to prioritise your list is to build a prioritisation matrix. To prepare your matrix, the stakeholders should collaborate on answering six questions for each decision in your list. If the decisions were documented correctly, most of this information should be readily available.

The first two questions relate to how the work will be evaluated and how you'll know whether it's been successful:

1. **Which primary objectives and business metrics is this decision expected to impact?** This question ensures that the decision is linked to your strategy.

2. **How much does the decision cost and what is its measurable impact on those business objectives?** The cost is typically the easier of the two answers to find. Simply counting the number of people in the team and the costs of the licences for the systems that they use will give you a feel for how much it costs to make the key decisions in that team. The tougher metric to calculate is the corresponding impact on the strategic objective – this is what is also known as the attributed return. If this

information is hard to come by, then, typically, a separate attribution return calculation is required. This information is critical to identifying which cases to focus on; you must be able to articulate how the business will know whether the work invested in this decision has been worth it. Since it's essential that your data initiatives show a demonstrable impact, it's a good idea to select decisions that are easy to measure. Be clear about what should be implemented to measure the impact, together with the technical effort required to do so.

The next two questions help assess the impact of the work:

3. **How big is the expected or desired impact?** This helps provide an understanding of the expected attributed return.

4. **How often is the decision made?** Decisions that occur more frequently will naturally multiply the overall impact of the data investment.

Finally, the last questions help you get a feel for how much investment will be needed to develop the solution:

5. **How much will it cost to develop the solution?** Expensive solutions to decisions can be worthwhile even if the improvement is modest, but you'll need to understand the trade-offs.

6. **How long will it take to develop the solution?**
   Understanding the time required from the technical and business teams involved will be critical to prioritisation. When will the organisation be able to realise benefits from the work involved? Use cases that can be solved quickly are good for maintaining buy-in on your data initiative efforts.

Next, to develop the prioritisation matrix, answers to the above questions should be divided into three clear metrics:

1. **ROI** (questions 2, 3, 4 and 5)

2. **Time to market** (question 6)

3. **Technical difficulty** (questions 2, 5 and 6)

Using these metrics, you can develop a hotspot analytical graph (see next page) that indicates which decisions should be addressed first. This graph contains two axes: one for technical difficulty and the other for time to market. Both are measured on a scale of 1 to 10, with 1 being low and 10 being high.

You can see in the matrix that decisions that are technically easier to develop move further to the right on the x-axis. We plot those decisions that we expect to benefit from most quickly higher up the y-axis. The size of each circle indicates the attributed return.

In our example above, decision 3 would be a great place to start, possibly followed by decisions 6 and 5.

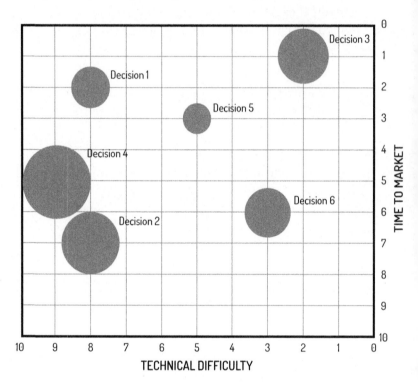

The use case prioritisation matrix

Note that decisions 2 and 4 are represented by large circles, meaning their ROI is high, yet during analysis it was determined that they were both technically difficult to develop, and time to market is relatively long.

Early success is important. Therefore, organisations should seek to develop data solutions for the least controversial decisions that also are the quickest and least technically difficult. These decisions will appear in the top right quadrant of your hotspot graph.

Remember: quick wins are good for obtaining and maintaining buy-in. If your data team is new and inexperienced, starting small gives them a few projects to sharpen their skills on.

However, each organisation operates differently and, depending on your climate and culture, you might decide to go ahead and tackle those big ROI items sooner rather than later. While good prioritisation still requires judgement, creating this matrix will give you the objective, hard data needed to avoid prioritising based solely on political reasons or gut feelings.

CREATE THE EXECUTION PLAN

A huge prerequisite to any execution plan must be an evaluation of the organisation's current state and its ability to execute it. Where are you starting? What tools, knowledge and resources are already available for executing the plan? Which do you need to obtain or develop?

To build a road map to your destination, you need to know where you are in the process. Giving a driver an instruction to turn left to reach a certain destination assumes knowledge of where the driver is at that specific point in time. If the driver is not where you expect them to be or not facing the direction you assume, the instruction to turn left could take them to a completely wrong destination. The same applies to a big-data strategy. You need to know what the existing capabilities are within the organisation to design the road map to solve the defined use cases.

The capability assessment

To understand the current state of play, you'll need a structured approach to assess the state of each of the fundamental components discussed up to this point. You'll need to know how well the organisation has been set up to create knowledge, insight or sophisticated algorithms as well as how prepared the business is to use them. This is called a capability assessment and there are several approaches to carrying this out, from detailed questionnaires through to long-winded workshops and documentation. Over the last couple of years, however, I've developed a simplified structured methodology that allows organisations to quickly understand how well they are set up to deliver value from data. In an effort to keep things simple, I call it the data value model.

This model shows that the ingredients described in this book need to converge to maximise two things: what the data can do and what it is used for.

Key #1 summarised that there are essentially five key things that you should do with data:

1. Understand what happened

2. Understand why it happened

3. Predict what is likely to happen

4. Prescribe a solution

5. Automatically decide and execute the next course of action

Each of these increases in sophistication the further down the list you go, but they also increase in value.

The first part of the model uses all of the keys to increase the sophistication of what you can do with data.

The second part looks at what you can use these outputs for, ie, there's a reason why you want to know what has happened, predict and prescribe a solution. As mentioned in Key #1, data's only use case is decisions. Therefore, the second part of the model focuses on increasing an understanding of where data can be used. Together, these two areas of focus form the back-bone of a co-ordinate grid or a two-by-two matrix, as seen below.

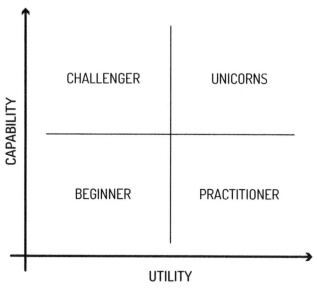

The data value model

The y-axis measures the technical capabilities and the sophistication of what you can do with data and the x-axis measures how well the output of the data (or knowledge and insight) is being used for key decisions as well as how well your leadership team is set up to maximise the use of data. Advancement along the x-axis means that the organisation is getting closer to understanding its key decisions (both internal and external) that can be automated with data.

The grid splits into four quadrants, representing the various positions an organisation, department or individual can occupy. By understanding which of the four quadrants the organisation is in, the set of activities required to deliver the use cases become clear.

The y-axis: Data output sophistication

Finding where your organisation scores on the y-axis simply requires an honest assessment of the sophistication of the data output being produced. A quick way to assess this is to ask whether the knowledge or insight the organisation produces is more a result of hindsight or foresight.

- **Hindsight** naturally takes the form of standard ad hoc reporting, dashboards, alerts and queries. The knowledge produced typically answers questions such as: 'What happened in the previous quarter?' 'How many users joined last month?' 'What have they bought, and why?'

  While these might seem like obvious business intelligence (BI) questions, the world of data science and big data does a lot to enhance the scope of questions that can be asked. For example, BI could give us knowledge about the total sales for last month, whereas data science can give us knowledge about the overall sentiment of the brand among a specific cohort of society. While this is considered hindsight, it's advanced and can only be achieved through new technologies and techniques that are used in data science. Your typical BI analyst would not be able to provide you with this sort of knowledge without the benefits of data science.

- **Foresight**, on the other hand, is what data science is most commonly known for. It's the ability to use a range of data sources to predict certain outcomes. For example, a typical data science prediction algorithm can be used to determine which customers have a good chance of moving to a competitor and when this is likely to occur. This would be valuable knowledge for teams that oversee retention.

  Furthermore, data science provides an additional stage beyond pure foresight. For example, using big data, it can provide the retention team with additional insight into exactly what they should do to influence the user to remain loyal. For some organisations, the idea that data science can give you predictive knowledge is already quite futuristic, and the notion that it can also influence the action of a customer may seem far-fetched. However, science has already proven that, together with a range of other variables (or environmental variables), human beings make decisions to act using both information and knowledge. Therefore, provision of the right knowledge to the right individual at the right time will significantly influence the decisions they make.

The x-axis: Decision intelligence

Plotting along the x-axis for how your organisation uses its data output requires an understanding of the key decisions that have been identified as part of the use-case decision discovery. Often, organisations are misaligned in this area; on one end of the spectrum, they are producing amazing but irrelevant insights because the decisions are not clear. On the other hand, the decisions are clear but the data science teams are not delivering effective analytics. The x-axis is where assessors score the usage of the knowledge that is being produced in line with the defined use cases. The further right you go, the more strategic decisions are being automated by using data.

Plotting the company's position using these axes will effectively allocate the company to one of the four quadrants. Let's consider each up close.

The Beginners

This is the starting position for most traditional organisations that do not routinely collect and store the data available today. Typically, Beginners still wrestle with standard reporting and business infor-mation. Perhaps the business doesn't trust the data it has and so hardly uses it. It's likely that it does not yet have a senior individual in a leadership position to push for behaviour change or drive the data strategy deep into the business, and it's unlikely that it has a data science team in place to increase the sophistication of the data output.

In this quadrant, we can also expect poor alignment or understanding of the organisational strategy and desired direction of the company, a lack of KPIs, disparate analytics and data positioned as an IT function apart from the business, and a struggle to establish a single version of truth. Some may be looking to consultants to execute expensive eighteen-month projects to get them to the next stage by building large-scale data warehouses.

Overall, usage of any existing data is ineffective, and the data output is not advanced enough to see big game-changing benefits.

The Challengers

With Challengers, there's likely to be a sophisticated, expensive team in place, but the environment is usually a little hostile. You might hear these remarks in the meeting rooms of a Challenger organisation: 'We don't know what the data science team does' and 'They're a really expensive team but we're not seeing any return.'

Organisations can end up in this stage because of failed implementation and have essentially taken a step backward. Or, they jump onto the data science hype wagon, investing large amounts of money and resources before developing and prioritising practical use cases.

These organisations have a good idea of what you can do with data as evidenced by their output, but they are uncertain as to where in the business these outputs should be used to maximise value. With such a technical team, there is a good chance that the focus is more on algorithm maximisation rather than concern for ROI.

The Practitioners

Organisations or individuals in the Practitioner quadrant put the available data output to good use. Similar to Beginners, the data output primarily reviews the past with a focus on what happened, with some determination of why but, differently to the Beginners, they use the output effectively. Start-ups with strict adherence to tight budgetary controls often occupy this quadrant because many of them need data to make quick decisions on what is working or not working.

Practitioners have the greatest potential to move into the Unicorn quadrant – the most valuable quadrant (MVQ) – because they already use much of the day-to-day data they collect. Moving into the MVQ is basically a technology-related effort, so it's possible that what's preventing Practitioners from becoming Unicorns is a shortage of suitable skills.

The Unicorns

The Unicorn quadrant is the MVQ of the four. Unicorn organisations are winning at the data puzzle game; they're extracting maximum value from their data.

Every business should strive to enter the MVQ. This requires a thorough grasp of strategy and the key contributing decisions. They have done enough work on their key decisions to attribute the cost and corresponding return to each decision. They know the relationships and have even modelled the impact and choices for these decisions. The right amount of data is being produced and critical decisions are being made automatically based on sound data science. In the MVQ, data science is truly generating value for the organisation because the sophisticated data output being created is utilised for clear business purposes aligned with strategic goals. It's truly resulting in value to the organisation in terms of ROI and business growth.

Moving around the quadrants needs all of the keys mentioned in this book. You will have noticed that you can move from a Beginner to a Challenger by simply adding a more advanced team (covered in the next chapter). However, as discussed, the Challenger quadrant is an undesirable one. The focus should be on *relevant* sophistication, and relevance can only increase with a greater shift to the right. In turn, this can only happen when data is demystified, a leader is in place, a game plan is developed and the culture of the organisation has been transformed. This does not give the team a free pass as they too can be blockers for a successful cultural shift. To better understand the right composition of team required to ensure a movement in the right direction, let's move on to the next key – build the right data team.

KEY #4
Building Data Teams

Despite all the amazing advances in analytical techniques and supporting technology, the process of building a big-data team remains a difficult and time-consuming task. The main reason for this challenge is frequently changing technology. Once-popular solutions dating from 2010 are dying a slow death, with more recent technologies making things faster and easier by addressing the problems of their predecessors. Another reason is that many have not fully realised the enterprise nature of data, ie, it is complex with many interconnected moving parts. Finally, a lack of clarity exists around the exact skills required to work with data, specifically the role of the DS – the mythical creature every organisation strives to hire who can, single-handedly, 'automagically' develop and execute your data proposition.

To set up an effective data team, we need to understand three important criteria:

- The enterprise nature of data
- The skills required to deliver effective solutions
- How they are set up in an organisation

DATA AS AN ENTERPRISE APPLICATION

Rarely do we hear about the enterprise nature of data – and this is a problem. Enterprise software is completely different than your standard application and requires an alternative approach to deploy successfully.

The term 'enterprise' typically refers to highly complex cross-organisational business systems that:

- Address requirements of multiple users
- Require multiple components
- Use extensive parallel processing with complex logic

Examples of enterprise software include accounting software, CRM, BI systems and, today, 'big-data solutions'.

Often, enterprise applications satisfy a range of business requirements, where the solution for one of those requirements has a corresponding impact on other requirements in ways that are often difficult to understand. Any failure to meet just one of the requirements could spell disaster for the whole project. With big data, the process of identifying data, sourcing it, cleaning it, preparing it for analysis, and sometimes effecting decisions 'on the fly' is complex. If there is an error in any of these parts of the process, the domino effect comes into play, migrating its way to the end solution. The algorithm may produce erroneous results – and identifying the root of the issue is rarely straightforward.

To add to the complexity, the requirements for enterprise applications usually involve encoding business processes, business policies and industry rules and regulations. The same goes for a big-data solution. For example, as we discussed earlier, there's increasing pressure from consumers regarding the use of personally identifiable data: how it's collected, what systems it's shared with or processed through, and even what analytics you can run through it.

Enterprise applications are also expected to be robust enough to sustain a continuous 'always on' operation while maintaining a high level of reliability and performance. They are often mission-critical, and must meet stringent requirements for security and administration, allowing for efficient maintenance and monitoring. Successful organisations are taking mission-critical decisions where big data and data science have a material impact. Ensuring that these systems are secure, reliable and always on is now an essential, non-functional requirement for any data solution.

With that, it is clear that data solutions *are* enterprise applications. They involve complex processes and must accommodate a host of rules and international regulations. The task of enterprise development is extraordinarily complex. Consequently, the team tasked with its execution must embrace a range of technical and non-technical skills that are hard to find in an individual.

Designing the team to address this challenge calls for a way to simplify this complexity, and that can only be done through a form of abstraction. Clustering these requirements into categories of similar require-ments condenses the problem into a set of more manageable tasks and reveals how they depend on one another. When you understand the interactions between groups of requirements, you can tackle them systematically, understanding the skills required, bal-ancing and adjusting each requirement as you build the solution.

The six categories below represent such an abstraction for data, each describing a set of requirements for the successful development of every big-data solution.

Category	Requirements related to...
Business	Business goals, data use cases, execution plan, business rules, policies and industry regulations. Includes total costs, investment sizing and ROI expectations.
User	The consumer of the output: internal and external users, machine and human. Includes deployment, A/B testing, experimentation, training, documentation and service-level agreements where necessary.
Data	The type of data required, where it's sourced, how it's extracted and how often it should be available and accessed.
Architecture	The physical application architecture, distribution, engineering and interconnection of components, and the processing and storage of data.
Machine Learning	The selection, design, training, building and testing of algorithms.
Engineering	The engineering and production of algorithms into new and or existing products.

Enterprise solutions are complex so, inevitably, business requirements interact with the other requirements by acting as a point of reference for each category, and they are brought to reality for the end user by meeting the requirements in the user category. Data requirements interact mainly with the architecture, but also impact the machine-learning techniques and approach for engineering. The machine-learning approach combined with the intricacies defined in the user requirements will have a significant impact on engineering. Such a complex interplay between the ranges of requirements is a natural feature of an enterprise solution and is not unique to big data.

The next task for an enterprise solution is the process of finding the people to deliver each set of requirements. Finding one person to address all these requirements is not impossible but is incredibly difficult. Yet many organisations are doing just that. This search for that mythical creature – the DS – has become one of industry's biggest contemporary problems.

THE PROBLEM WITH THE MYTHICAL DATA SCIENTIST

The meaning of 'data scientist' varies, depending on who you ask. When a commonly used term lacks a precise definition, different expectations will be placed on it, causing much confusion in the marketplace. As a result, locating the right person with the right combination of skills and getting them to do the right activities is a formidable challenge. This lack of clarity leads to a meagre supply of those who truly possess the required skills, and in an industry where there is limited supply of skills, but the demand and willingness to invest in those skills are high, we see a growing 'grey market' of pretenders claiming to understand your needs and promising to provide the magic solution.

There's an increasing number of new organisations, recruiters and individuals calling themselves experts in data science, masters of this mysterious art. They prey on organisations that are desperate to be involved in the data puzzle but don't know enough to separate the wheat from the chaff.

Finding a true DS is difficult – you need only look at a typical job description to understand the breadth and depth of skills and experience they are expected to have.

To illustrate this, I analysed over thirty of the top data science jobs posted on LinkedIn. I found over fifty different required key skills and grouped them into the following clusters:

1. **Advanced analytics** – mathematical modelling, research techniques at PhD level, statistics and mathematics, machine learning, pattern recognition/learning, uncertainty, data mining,

algorithm design and the experimental method, graph theory, complex system analysis, machine learning and AI

2. **Software engineering** – software product development and a host of programming languages from Java and Python to shell scripting and Ruby

3. **Databases** – a range of database and data-engineering concepts such as data warehousing and structures of data, schemas, data tools and technologies such as Hadoop, SQL, structured and unstructured data storage, data processing, data management, visualisation and ETL

4. **Commercial awareness** – an understanding of consumer behaviour, marketing and consumer relationship management, communication skills, intellectual curiosity, human computer interaction, domain knowledge for the industry, good communication and an ability to interact with technical people of other disciplines as well as non-technical people

5. **Computer systems** – advanced computing, high-performance computing, data mining, big-data platforms and the cloud

'Advanced analytics' features in all the job descriptions, with 'machine learning' or other terms from the realm of statistics also appearing regularly. However, the DS is also expected to write enterprise-level code and build products as a software engineer – not just as a standard developer, but as an enterprise-grade engineer sufficiently familiar with the nuances of big data to build a production system that has access to the required data in a timely fashion and that is robust enough to interact with potentially millions of users.

The expectations don't stop there. When it comes to database concepts, DSs are expected to understand how databases operate in the same way that a seasoned database administrator and database scripting expert would. This person is expected to understand data architecture and environment to support the desired extraction methods, storage, processing and cleaning of data.

Moreover, the DS is expected to work with business users at all levels, using their commercial know-how to understand marketing, human computer interaction and purchasing behaviour to ensure the most effective delivery of their big-data product. Finally, to support this wide-ranging brief, the DS needs a strong in-depth understanding of their respective industry – often referred to as a strong foundation of domain knowledge – to build effective machine-learning algorithms.

If you step back from the detail of these expectations for a moment, you'll realise that they align directly to the six enterprise-level requirements needed to deliver a big-data solution.

- Advanced analytics cluster → Machine-learning requirements

- Software engineering cluster → Engineering requirements

- Databases cluster → Data requirements

- Commercial awareness cluster → Business requirements and user requirements

- Computer systems cluster → Architecture requirements

From this, we see that this mythical DS – as an individual – is expected to be an expert in each area of the entire spectrum of enterprise requirements. *Really?*

Incidentally, mediocrity in any one of the requirement categories will spell doom for the data project because of the high-dependency relationship between all the components.

These areas require dramatically different skills, education and training, with very little overlap. It's easy to see how such a wide range of specialties can be confusing for applicants, employers and project owners, significantly increasing the risk to the success of the product. The maxim 'jack of all trades, master of none' applies here, and not as a compliment. The field of data science seems to want to be all things to all people, and with a lack of a precise definition, it's failing more often than not.

I have yet to meet a DS with the required level of expertise in every one of these areas. A majority of those that I encounter today have strong machine-learning skills but are weaker in engineering and database skills. I have met others that were strong data engineers with expertise in deploying complex solutions with large amounts of data and complex calculations in a timely manner but are light on machine-learning knowledge and experience. Most DSs that I meet are weakest in commercial and business interaction skills. It seems that, somewhat stereotypically, those with strong numerical skills tend not to excel in communication and social interactions – and these folks are put in a room with non-technical business experts of all levels, expected to run ideation workshops and navigate sometimes politically stormy waters to elicit requirements, prioritise and suggest commercially useful opportunities.

For this reason, the data science talent gap is wide, with the demand for the right expertise largely outweighing the supply. The gap isn't likely to be closed any time soon, so companies must work hard to find employees with the skills to make a big-data project work.

The other extreme would be to find six individuals, each an expert in one of the six enterprise skill requirements. This may seem like overkill, but organisations should focus more on fulfilling the skills mix by assembling a team that is greater than the sum of its parts. Until this concept is embraced by senior executives, companies will continue to fail at cracking the data code.

KEY ROLES AND REQUIRED SKILLS

To understand the key roles and supporting skills needed for an effective big-data team, we must first recognise the fact that while we have six different categories of enterprise requirements, the skills required to deliver them will have some degree of overlap. For example, the skills required to deliver the business and user enterprise needs are similar, as are the data and architecture requirements. However, machine learning and engineering have less of an overlap.

Overlaps between skill sets are important because the greater the overlap the greater the opportunity to consolidate the activities, reducing the total number of roles required to deliver the six categories of requirement. Based on the overlaps identified earlier, big data therefore needs a minimum number of four skill sets, or roles:

1. **Business analyst,** who covers the business requirements and user requirements categories

2. **Data engineer,** who covers data requirements and architecture requirements

3. **Data scientist**, whose scope of expertise is limited to machine-learning requirements and other advanced analytics

4. **Data science engineer**, who covers engineering requirements

At this point smaller companies or startups should not be alarmed; it is ideal to have an individual in each of these areas, but in a startup or a smaller company, where many people wear multiple hats, you should focus on what each of these roles do and the skill sets they require. This allows you to consider individuals in other areas of your business to see if you already have those skills in place.

Let's consider each in relation to the requirements categories that they should address.

The business analyst

The skills required to address the business and user requirements categories have been in use long before big data came along. These individuals perform a crucial function, essentially covering the beginning stages and the implementation of your big-data deliverable, frequently interacting with every member of the team during the project. We typically know them as business analysts, or BAs.

Their involvement at the start of the project begins by being heavily involved in the production of the data game plan, which is a key component of the business requirements category. As we saw in the previous chapter, the game plan will need an understanding of the business objectives, the big-data use cases, the execution plan and an initial view of the costs, investment requirements and expected ROI.

To do this, BAs are required to review reams of corporate strategy documents and run workshops and interview sessions to tease out important information about the business and the corresponding industry it operates in. They need to build an understanding of the true business goals, identify the core decisions that must be made inside and outside of the organisation and start the process of identifying big-data use cases.

Another important part of this role is interacting with individuals across all levels of the organisation at all levels, helping the data leader create and maintain a data-driven culture, so excellent communication skills are paramount. In fact, the BA will need to have a range of soft skills including patience, relationship building, the ability to communicate effectively with people who don't speak the same 'language' and the ability to deal with ambiguity. Especially at the beginning of big-data projects, there can be a lot of ambiguity around strategic goals and what big data is expected to do. The BA is expected to help cut through multiple interpretations and clearly articulate what the data will do as well as how, when and who will be involved. The BA must be diligent in teasing out information from stakeholders.

The BA must be able to accommodate new information that surfaces later than we'd like (and it will). The BA will need to facilitate workshops, ask the right questions, listen to the answers and absorb what's being said, evaluating multiple options before helping the team settle on a solution.

While discovering the key decisions that must be made and the problems that must be solved, the BA must not only listen to stakeholder needs but also critically consider those needs by asking probing questions until the *real* need is surfaced and understood.

All this requires strong communication, critical thinking and problem-solving skills.

The BA must also collaborate with other data team members to devise an execution plan that can be measured and monitored throughout the duration of the project. With legal restrictions around the use of data and privacy concerns, the BA will need to clearly communicate constraints within which the project is expected to operate, including business rules, policies and industry regulations such as rules governing consumer privacy and opt-in laws in different countries.

This interaction with architects, DSs and engineers will continue throughout the project, with the BA serving as a useful conduit between developments in the big-data team and the rest of the organisation. This function is critical since most organisations need regular education, excitement and enablement around big data, and the BA is ideally placed to meet those needs.

The BA will be involved in all the requirements categories during the project duration, facilitating teams, solving technical challenges and effectively being the business representative for technical stakeholders and the technical representative for business stakeholders – in other words, they are the liaison between the business and technical sides of the project. Therefore, the BA must forge strong relationships with everyone that has anything to contribute to or will be affected by the project. This involves building trust and stepping into a leadership role to bridge gaps and ensure that all the enterprise requirements are being met.

Among the four key roles, the BA is the least technical. Instead, this role requires a strong analyst who understands how to collect, extract and infer conclusions from data. They will be expected to use a variety of techniques to

- analyse problems and possible solutions
- identify gaps that others gloss over

- anticipate the downstream impact of a change or new solution

Any big-data initiative will produce outputs that must be tested and verified from both analytical and technical perspectives. When an algorithm is produced, the BA is tasked with verifying its output from an analytical perspective by tapping into their domain knowledge to determine whether it's producing the right result. The technical and mathematical development of an algorithm can appear to be correct, but domain expertise is necessary for the identification of any anomalies.

For example, at JustGiving, we trained a machine to determine the best images to use for a charity fundraising campaign so that we could advise our users on what pictures they should use to maximise the donations on their fundraising pages. The machine determined that fundraising pages with pictures of *bicycles* raise significantly more than any other image. All the mathematics checked out. Our product would have recommended to our millions of fundraisers that they should use pictures of bicycles to increase donations to their fundraising page. It's only because of the internal domain knowledge of those capturing the requirements that we were able to identify this as an incorrect outcome. It turned out that fundraisers who used cycling events to raise money raised more on average by using the image of a bicycle. With this knowledge, the algorithm was rerun, this time controlling for the event type to avoid such biases.

This generally underappreciated reality that effective BAs need intimate domain knowledge is a cog in the wheel for many who attempt to solve the data puzzle. Someone who understands your industry and can create and answer pertinent questions will be able to identify anomalies that can't be discovered by looking at the numbers alone. It's important to understand how data affects revenue, profitability, lifetime value and a host of other factors important to the business.

The output from data science algorithms can be written for human or machine consumption. For example, take an algorithm that decides which email to send to a user. If the algorithm is expected to select an email without human intervention, then it's written for machine consumption, and the output of the data is focused on non-functional requirements around the latency of delivery, what to serve in the event of an error, efficiency tracking, monitoring and, of course, security. If, on the other hand, a human must make the decision based on the data, then the output is for human consumption and will need to be more intuitive, descriptive and, in some instances, supported by visualisation.

This is another opportunity for the BA to straddle the business and technical worlds to ensure that the resulting information is packaged in a way that can easily be consumed. The key skill here is being able to tell a story through data and providing good visualisation of that data. This skill is another core element in developing a data-driven culture, and another key ingredient in the recipe for data science success.

The data engineer

The role of the data engineer, or DE, is central to another requirements category: the data category. By delivering all that is required around data, the DE plays a pivotal role in supporting a data-driven culture. The DE's role is to oversee all aspects of the capture, processing, storage and accessibility of data.

This role begins with a collaborative effort to uncover opportunities for data acquisition from new and existing data sources to meet business requirements. The DE will need to determine how best to capture, clean and transform the data. This person must help identify gaps since big data is not necessarily perfect data – it will always need some cleaning and adjustments. The DE must also decide on how the data will be managed, stored, accessed, manipulated and scheduled. Think of DEs as the plumbers building the data pipeline, addressing problems associated with data capture, database integration, messy and incomplete data and unstructured or semi-structured data sets of varying types, sizes and schedules of availability.

Their ultimate aim is to provide clean, usable data that is optimised for consumption by whoever may require it, typically business users and DSs. The DE's goal for business users is to get the right amount of data into their hands at the right time to support timely decisions. And for the DSs, DEs work on processing a massive amount of data that allows DSs to train and build advanced algorithms in a secure and robust environment.

The DE is responsible for the development, construction, testing and maintenance of architectures, databases and large data-processing systems. Everything that they build must be scalable and in line with the business requirements and industry practices.

Any organisation that wants to build a suitable big-data environment will require a qualified DE who can

- select a platform

- design a technical architecture and test

- deploy the proposed solution

Choosing an architecture and building an appropriate big-data solution are challenging because so many factors must be considered. The solution will need to cater to the needs of the organisation as well as the DSs and data science engineers. Thus the impact of

DEs is significant. Their success lies in both the quality and the quantity of what they can offer.

To deliver these requirements, the DE needs to have a firm understanding of major programming/scripting languages such as Java, Linux, PHP, Ruby, Python and/or Scala, which are used for data ingestion from other providers and when they begin the process of joining systems together. (Which one is used is not terribly important, as long as it's embraced as a common language among your team.)

In addition, it's essential that the DE has experience in working with industry-standard extract, transform and load tools. They should have experience in designing solutions for multiple large data warehouses and a good understanding of cluster and parallel architecture as well as high-scale or distributed relational database management systems (RDBMS). Because of the requirement to work with unstructured data, it is important to have knowledge of NoSQL platforms.

From an architecture perspective, a successful DE should have a significant amount of experience of normal solutions architecture and application design, with an extensive amount of hands-on experience before making the move to big-data solutions. About ten years of work experience is common for this position, including experience with major big-data solutions and offerings from the likes of Microsoft, Amazon and Google, and a strong background in information management and data processing on multiple platforms.

A vigilant DE will recommend ways to improve data reliability, efficiency and quality. With so much changing so quickly, it's essential that the DE keeps abreast of new data management technologies and software, including open-source options, and must not be afraid to integrate these into existing structures as appropriate. The DE should be judicious about tool selection and, once continuous pipelines are installed to and from the huge reservoirs of filtered information, both the business and DSs should be able to pull out relevant data sets for their respective purposes easily.

As with all members of the big-data team, DEs must have good collaboration skills. In addition to frequent collaboration with the data team to ensure alignment on project goals, a large part of their interactions will be with the consumers of the data, both business users and DSs, to determine which data are needed for analysis.

The communication between the DE and DS is especially vital. Data isn't just thrown into a database awaiting consumption; it must be optimised to the use case of the DS. Having a clear understanding of how this handshake occurs is important in reducing the errors in the data pipeline, and important considerations need to be made regarding how this is done.

Some DEs provide a platform for DSs to run SQL, others provide a reporting front end like Tableau, or prefer to provide access via an API. Whichever method is selected, it must allow the DSs to focus on what they have been hired to do rather than how to access or clean the data. It's not uncommon for DSs to spend 80% of their time cleaning data. The DE must reduce this effort by improving the quality of and access to the data so the DSs can begin working their advanced analytics and machine-learning magic as soon as possible.

The data scientist

Earlier in this chapter we determined that although it's a prevailing misconception in business today, DSs cannot be expected to be a master of all big-data roles, since no one person can possibly excel at the wide variety of knowledge and skills involved.

The job descriptions analysis described earlier revealed that advanced analytics (which includes mathematical modelling, statistics and machine learning) is the most frequently occurring requirement. Limiting the expectations of the DS to these skills is significantly more realistic.

As big data is the raw material required to produce knowledge, the DS is the alchemist of the twenty-first century – the person who can turn raw data into purified insights and knowledge. The DS is expected to develop machine-learning algorithms and crunch numbers to help answer questions and make predictions with data. Their primary function is to help organisations turn their volumes of big data into valuable and actionable knowledge using appropriate data science methods and tools.

Indeed, data science is not necessarily a new field *per se*, but it can be considered as an advanced level of data mining or analytics that is driven and automated by machine learning, computer science and big data combined with domain expertise.

DSs may sometimes be presented with big data without a particular business problem in mind. As we discussed earlier, it's recommended that your DS is allocated about 10% of time for discovery. In this case, the curious DS is expected to explore the data, come up with the right questions and provide interesting findings. This is tricky because to analyse the data, a strong DS should have a broad knowledge of different techniques in machine learning, data mining, statistics and big-data infrastructures.

Many machine-learning algorithms are essentially extensions of statistical modelling procedures, and the problem-solving skills of a DS require an understanding of traditional and new data analysis methods to build statistical models or discover patterns in data, for example creating a recommendation engine, diagnosing patients based on their similarities or finding patterns in fraudulent transactions.

This person is statistically minded, with experience in programming and building data models. They should have experience working with different data sets of different sizes and shapes and be able to run algorithms on large-size data effectively and efficiently. It's essential for them to be well versed in computer science fundamentals and basic programming, including experience with database technologies.

A good DS will stay up to date with any up-and-coming changes and be on top of news regarding the development of new tools, theory and algorithms. They regularly review research papers, blogs and conference videos, and participate in online communities to keep abreast of the latest trends.

However, theory knowledge alone will not help a DS choose good values for the sixteen parameters a standard implementation of a random forest uses. The default values are good to get started, but which parameters should be modified depending on your data? Feature extraction is one of the most important parts of machine learning. Different types of problems need various solutions.

Choosing the right features, algorithms and parameters is an art. It's more like karate than maths. It can't be learned from a book. It's learned by doing, by getting your hands dirty and applying algorithms to various data sets, by lots of trial and error and by having seen hundreds of successful applications.

Standard implementations of machine-learning algorithms are widely available through libraries/packages/APIs, but applying them effectively involves choosing a suitable model, a learning procedure to fit the data and an understanding of how parameters affect learning. In addition, the DS is expected to know the relative advantages and disadvantages of different approaches and the numerous 'gotchas' that can trip you up.

At the end of the day, a DS needs the skills not only to view and analyse the data, but also to manipulate it. A statistician who reviews and interprets a set of data is different from a DS who can change the code that collects the data in the first place.

Often, it's a small component that fits into a larger ecosystem of products and services. The DS needs to understand how these different pieces work together, communicate with them and build appropriate interfaces for your component that others will depend on.

A DS is nothing without creativity and an overall intellectual curiosity. Despite the stereotype of data being all about numbers and statistics, big data is a rapidly changing and expanding field that requires a certain open-mindedness and creativity. To innovate, a good DS must be able to look beyond what came before and explore new ideas.

The data science engineer

While we've established that skills for the DS include machine learning with some coding, we still need the resulting data products to be part of a production system. The engineering of a recommendation system that potentially millions of users are going to use requires a deeper understanding of application development and distributed architecture.

Popular examples include the Facebook feed, Amazon's recommendations system and the movie recommendations on Netflix. The individuals that build this part of the solution are not your typical DS, and neither are they your standard developer; they are engineers who carefully design systems to deliver data solutions that avoid bottlenecks and allow algorithms to scale with increasing volumes of data.

The data science engineer (DSE) ensures consistent packing and release of code and data from one environment to the next, maintaining clear auditability and version control to understand which output corresponds to the code used to generate it. Software engineering best practices (including requirements analysis, system design, modularity, version control, testing, documentation, etc) are invaluable for productivity, collaboration, quality and maintainability.

It's also important that the DSE develops a clear roll-back strategy that's only a few clicks away. DSEs prepare for the worst by developing a failover strategy with validation procedures to maintain stability.

The skills needed in an effective DSE are similar to those of a strong software engineer or developer. However, when it comes to big data, an added layer of complexity is the requirement to understand distributed computing, cloud architectures, data movement and data storage. This is what makes DSEs unique compared to other software engineers, and this role is critical to establishing and utilising a successful big-data solution.

KEY #5

Creating A Culture For Success

As described earlier, the output generated from data must be used for key business or customer decisions to realise its true value yet, interestingly, ensuring that the output from data actually gets used is not as easy as it sounds. A truly data-driven culture must be established in the organisation to ensure that your data initiative results in high ROI and game-changing success.

Some years ago, I worked on a predictive model to increase the click-through rates of an email campaign. Despite demonstrating that the model would increase the click-through rates by more than 92% and significantly decrease the number of email recipients opting out, it was never used. This puzzled me. Why would this company commission the project yet, despite such clear, undeniable evidence, not use the model for the email campaigns? After suffering a small crisis in confidence, I began to observe the general behaviour of others in the organisation to understand how decisions were generally made.

It's probably not surprising that decisions were made primarily based on 'gut feelings' and experience. The team leader had years of experience and was selecting users to email based purely on intuition and what *seemed* to have worked previously. What was shocking, though, was finding that even the supposed successes were mere assumptions with no metrics applied. Generally, they celebrated the sending of the email but paid little or no attention to the corresponding results of what it was intended to achieve – forcing me to remind them that you cannot improve what you don't measure.

Such behaviour was not limited to this team, but as it was unintentionally rewarded, other teams began to follow suit.

I have encountered other examples of organisational behaviour where data will have no chance of thriving. In such organisations, the output from data is filed in a cabinet labelled 'Interesting Stuff From Data', where, sadly, it remains.

In some organisations, there is a desire to ask questions using data, but they are not necessarily the right questions, and I have seen backlogs of requests for data and analysis that mostly fit the interesting vs useful categories. It is not uncommon for executives to receive reports that they never open or, when they do, they simply scan them before deleting them so their contents have no impact on any subsequent decision making. In such organisations, you often get asked what the true value of the data team is. Questions get asked about what it 'does' and the attribution to value is difficult.

In other organisations, the requirement to capture data is always a nice-to-have requirement rather than a necessity. If any of these behaviours sound familiar, then your organisation needs to invest in building a data-driven culture, otherwise generating value from data will be nearly impossible.

The culture of an organisation sets the behaviours, values and expectations of how data is used, democratised and respected across every business unit or department. As a result, the organisational culture has a significant impact on the value that can be extracted from data. To optimise this value, organisations need to create an environment that encourages and rewards the increased use of the output derived from data over blind hunches and gut instinct. I am not suggesting here that it is a binary choice between 'use data' or 'gut' – data in itself can contain mistakes – what I am advocating is a behaviour that recognises our human biases and inefficiencies and thereby supplements decision making with data, establishing a healthy balance between gut-based and data-driven decisions.

A significant number of studies show a clear correlation between a company's predisposition to rely on data for decisions and its success in many core aspects such as profitability, increased employee engagement and the ability to innovate and find new sources of revenue.

One recent report showed that organisations with strong evidence of a data-driven culture saw an average 27% increase in revenue year on year compared to 7% for non-data-driven organisations. Additionally, 83% improved their process cycle times, compared with 39%, and 12% reduced operating expenses, compared with 1%.[5] These are just some of the benefits that can be expected in a data-driven culture.

It's therefore no surprise that the term 'data driven' has become a popular buzzword that, unfortunately, suffers the same fate as 'big data' in that it's not fully understood. A similar barrage of noise litters this definition. What exactly does it mean to be a data-driven organisation? Gartner defines this as businesses that use data 'to organize activities, make decisions, and resolve conflict.' Put simply, a data-driven

---

5   'The executives guide to effective analytics', Analyst Insight, Aberdeen Group, December 2013, available at http://cruconanalytics.com/wp-content/uploads/2014/02/Aberdeen-C-Suite-Guide-to-effective-analytics.pdf

organisation is one that makes decisions based on the right balance of gut, intuition and data analytics.

There seems to be universal agreement that being a data-driven organisation plays a crucial role in realising success in cracking the data code. However, without knowing exactly what such a culture looks like, we cannot understand its connections to other key elements of the organisation, nor can we develop good approaches to extracting maximum value from data. If we can define what a data-driven culture looks like, we'll better understand how to diagnose problems and achieve the game-changing results of a successful data initiative.

HALLMARKS OF A DATA-DRIVEN CULTURE

In a data-driven organisation, reliance on data is second nature. It's integrated into the organisation's way of thinking, deciding and working. Two things stick out when you enter a data-driven organisation: the overall behaviour of employees and the general working environment.

Employee characteristics

Data-driven organisations tend to have many employees passionate about the value of data, applying it to their decision making and spending time in dashboards, spreadsheets and reports. They're keen on identifying metrics or adding tracking to their activities so that they get to a more informed position.

To illustrate the different behaviours from the employees, consider two possible reactions to a scenario in which an organisation experienced a surge in the number of support calls.

- **Gut-based reaction**: 'I just overheard a help-desk call complaining about the new version of the product that we released, and it feels like there has been a sudden surge in the number of help-desk calls. This must be due to problems with the release of the new version. We need to roll back to the previous version as soon as possible.'

- **Data-driven reaction**: 'Over the last five months, we have seen a steady increase of roughly 6% month over month in the number of help-desk calls. Since the release of the latest version, the growth rate has remained constant. But the total number of calls related to the new version make up less than 0.5% and analysis of those calls shows that all but one of them are from the same individual. It doesn't look like we have a problem with the new version, and we should leave it in place. Let's take a closer look at the data to figure out what is causing the increase.'

The difference between the two reactions is stark but not uncommon today, as many organisations are still on this journey to becoming data driven. The gut-based reaction went straight to assumptions; there was no mention of, or attempt to access, data, to ask for some analysis or to probe further with specific questions. The gut-based reaction reached a conclusion that would most likely cause some catastrophic problems and confusion. Conversely, the data-driven response was based on data and resulted in a completely different suggestion.

Many data-driven organisations have their own approach and sequence for the way they do things, but they all display these five characteristics to some degree:

1. They consider the relationship between objectives and decisions

2. Their communication is based on facts

3. They're hungry for relevant data

4. They rely on testing and learning

5. They're data literate

Let's consider each characteristic in detail.

Objectives and decisions

Employees in a data-driven organisation are clear about what they're attempting to move and how it relates to the organisational strategy. The strategic objectives of the organisation are clearly articulated, and you can measure how well the organisation is progressing with well-defined KPIs. Employees are clear on the objectives and targets to be reached. When an objective is assigned to a team or person, they have identified and understood the leading indicators or, put simply, the initial measurable impact of the things that they do, allowing them to assess progress and determine whether they are on track for meeting their objectives. Consequently, this also allows them to have a better view of their contribution to organisational strategy, resulting in a motivated workforce keen to keep momentum going in the right direction. You find that they continually ask themselves

- What are the decisions that I need to make?

- What data do I need to make them?

- How are these decisions connected to the objectives and to other decisions?

By asking these questions as you go up the hierarchy, you will identify senior executives who can see very clearly whether a division or department is effective. This means that the attributed return on the business decisions is also clear to the senior team, enabling the company to make quicker, more profitable and better targeted decisions while maintaining a consistent approach to decision making across the organisation. The company becomes significantly more agile, making decisions and adapting at the same time.

Fact-based communication

Whenever someone offers an opinion, suggestion or an idea, it's accompanied by numbers and data – even though numbers may be imprecise at least there is some repeatable rationale being used. By focusing on fact-based insights, the number of arguments and debates within teams and among senior executives will decrease significantly and the reliance solely on 'gut instinct' – the fairly nebulous concept that traditionally drove both decisions and disagreements – also decreases.

More individuals within a data-driven organisation are empowered regardless of their experience. Julie Arsenault puts it so well: '"Do you have data to back that up?" should be a question that no one is afraid to ask (and everyone is prepared to answer).'[6] It becomes easy to bring ideas to the table when they're supported by the data. This also improves staff morale since the process by which their ideas can be heard is transparent and more democratic.

---

6 www.pagerduty.com/blog/how-to-create-a-data-driven-culture

Finally, numbers are communicated even if they illustrate poor performance. When the organisation experiences below-average performance, nobody tries to hide it, enabling teams to identify areas that need improvement. Decisions are based on numbers and facts and not on biases, preconceived notions or beliefs.

This trait tends to appear when employees have humbly understood that, in human nature, there are hundreds of biases that influence and cloud our decision making and so in an information-heavy world we must strive to include information to adjust for many of these natural biases.

Hunger for relevant data

All employees have access to the figures representing their team's activities as well as the organisation's. As such, all team members have a strong, fact-based understanding of the state of play for their respective teams or projects. Business users access reporting tools regularly and build spreadsheets to ask questions, explore, make decisions and prepare progress reports.

When starting something new, they're always keen to understand how they will be able to access and see performance data. Initiatives are not launched without the ability to measure as they communicate with metrics. For online projects, before the first line of code is written, data is collected to ensure that, on launch, it is available for analysis immediately.

Reliance on testing and learning

Knowledge and data can be elusive, and it's not always right at your fingertips. Data-driven organisations tend to have a strong testing culture and innovate through experimentation. Employees seek to run tests to discover what they don't know whenever possible. This is true of both online and offline businesses.

Relying on tests is second nature to employees. Before any corrective actions are taken for an entire audience or product, a test is carried out to check if this correction does indeed improve performance. As such, data justifies and validates projects for improvements and allows you to acquire a better understanding for further knowledge.

Finally, it's relatively non-confrontational. In a data-driven culture, it's OK to say, 'We don't know the answer, let's test it', then let the data shine. It becomes easy to be data critical, challenge assumptions, discuss and iterate.

Data literacy

In a data culture, staff are bilingual: analysts speak business and the business speaks data. Decision makers are data literate – meaning that they should have sufficient skills to judge good and poor experimental design, to push back on analysts when necessary, to ask the right questions and to interpret metrics and evidence appropriately.

It is vital here to stress that a data-driven culture does not by any means ignore gut instinct and experience. It only looks to strike a balance between human intuition and data – accepting the fact that intuition will always be influenced by individual biases.

Organisational set-up

One would be hard pressed to find an organisation today that doesn't have reports or dashboards all over their business, but this alone doesn't make them data driven. For many of these organisations, the reports are hardly opened, the dashboards always need another feature added before they can be considered useful, and both tend to be backward-looking, only reflecting what has already happened. Few can understand through their metrics *why* something happened, and even fewer are able to determine what is *likely* to happen or what to do about it.

Employee behaviour is, in part, influenced by technology, training and the structure of the organisation. Leaders who have tried and failed to get their organisations to be more data driven generally cite a range of reasons, from poor access to data, complexity of analytics tools and long lead times for insights to the sometimes overprotective nature of the IT organisation limiting access to data and the multiple data silos that prevent full-spectrum analysis.

These technical constraints and limitations seem to be a reasonable argument for the preference of gut instinct and experience over data. This points to the fact that in addition to employee characteristics, there are a range of organisational characteristics of data-driven organisations.

Becoming a successful data-driven organisation begins with a commitment from the leadership team to deliver value from data, and the investment in hiring an effective data team with a dedicated leader who will democratise and build a data-literate workforce. This will prepare the organisation to exploit the deluge of data, information and knowledge that will be produced by DSs. Below, I detail the full set of attributes for which organisations should strive.

Commitment

Organisations with data-driven cultures have widespread commitment to achieving success with data, from top to bottom. Frontline managers, BAs and many others use data to do their jobs every day and they're supported by the tools, training and incentives they need to do so. Data-driven decision making becomes the standard way of working for everyone, and this behaviour is rewarded. The data produced is used on a regular basis, and everyone understands and is committed to the data initiative.

New roles, new titles

New roles are created with new responsibilities, and someone is responsible for the quality, collection and accessibility of the data.

Today, we see two roles in particular: the CDO and the CAO (see Key #2 for a description of these two positions). Organisations with these roles in place demonstrate that they view data as an essential asset. However, the mere existence of these roles in the organisation is not enough. These roles must be tied directly to senior leadership to unleash full transformational potential of data science in action across the business.[7]

High-quality, easily accessible data

Quality data is in the hands of all users across the organisation. Consumers of the data trust it and are able to use the tools in place to access the data for exploratory analysis, canned and custom reports and dashboards. Everyone can easily access data that

---

7   http://bigdata.teradata.com/GB/Big-Ideas/Data-Driven-Culture/

relates to them and figures representing their team's activities. All team members have a precise understanding of both the strengths and weaknesses of the team as a result of the data.

Organisations that are successful with their big-data endeavours run their data teams as a centralised centre of excellence reporting to the executive champion. This is an essential shift and should come part and parcel with the introduction of a role at the executive level who can promote the cause.

In an organisation where business users are aware of what information is available, how to access the data they require and use it to influence an outcome, the value of data rapidly increases. A data-driven organisation should democratise data as much as possible, providing staff with the data and skills they need to be effective, embed data into their processes and become empowered to make appropriate data-driven decisions.

Openness and sharing

Data-driven companies have a lack of data silos. Instead, to ensure data is recent and relevant, they collate information from across the organisation. Centralising data allows for constant updates, keeping data fresh and up to date throughout the business.

Goals first

Employees are not only clear about their own goals and objectives, but they're also clear on those of the organisation. Leadership communicates the company's mission, vision and strategy. They are documented and communicated to the entire organisation, and everyone is enabled, incentivised and rewarded for using data to make informed decisions and fulfilling strategic goals.

Train and reward non-data staff

Each employee has been trained on data analysis and interpretation. As such, employees are more at ease with data interpretation, know which methods to employ and analyse and are empowered to act accordingly. Data is never used to point fingers in case of failure. However, when something does fail, data is shared in a neutral manner with the purpose of defining conditions for improved performance. As such, employees are less afraid to take potentially beneficial risks, and less hesitant to use data that might reveal less-than-stellar performance so it can be improved.

Learning and testing culture

You'll see a strong A/B culture in data-driven organisations, allowing them to innovate, learn, improve and try out new ideas, and get direct feedback from real customers and users. Hypothesis generation is rewarded and, importantly, it's recognised and accepted that anyone can generate a good idea. In my experience, organisations often use data to identify one-off business improvements, but those who are more data driven are committed to the discipline of continuous learning. In 2013, when I was at JustGiving, I met with Sir Clive Humby and he mentioned how every transaction involving a Tesco Clubcard is a chance to learn – which is clearly another reason why Tesco has been so successful with this approach.

Collecting (almost) everything

Validated data-collection projects have no trouble getting financed. Whenever and wherever it's possible to get new and useful data, the necessary budget is easily found, enabling stakeholders to make data-based decisions. Employees know that management fully values data and attributes high importance to it.

Strategically, operationally and culturally, data-driven organisations collect as much data as they can and use it in all aspects of the business. The reason for this is that you have no idea what hidden correlations or causal relationships that you may find. For example, most common variables used in credit-scoring models included income, bank balance, outstanding credit, payment history and employment status. However, a 'maths-loving' executive called JP Martin, from one of

Canada's largest retail chains – Canadian Tire – was able to work with large amounts of data to identify that purchase behaviour or the brands that people buy are strong predictors of their credit score. In fact, an article in the *New York Times* reported that a test of JP Martin's approach found it to be significantly more accurate than traditional approaches.[8] Such a finding would not have been possible if only the traditional data points had been captured.

But note the 'almost'. Earlier, we discussed how it's a good idea to focus on targeted data collection, especially in the early stages of your data campaign. We also discussed that it's a good idea to allow your data team to devote 10% of its time to exploration – and for exploration to have a good chance of turning up something useful, a wide array of data is necessary.

You need to know everything about your business. Space is cheap and we now have the luxury of storing more data than ever before in the search for data that will open new doors to success.

The habit of creating more knowledge

Data-driven organisations are in the habit of constantly creating knowledge and insights that are likely to be used, resulting in more information through

---

8 Duhigg, C, 'What does your credit card company know about you?' *The New York Times Magazine* (12 May 2009), available at www.nytimes.com/2009/05/17/magazine/17credit-t.html

employees' desire to learn and continually enhancing and improving the actionable information and knowledge that is generated, as shown below.

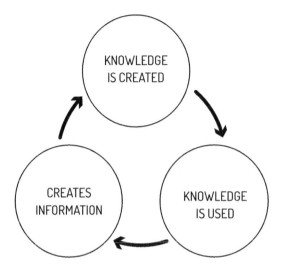

The virtuous circle of knowledge

This habit spreads throughout the organisation and the volume and types of knowledge created begin to grow as more parts of the organisation rely on it for decision making. This effectively creates a virtual cycle of knowledge and utility. Once this cycle has begun, organisations start to regularly operate in the MVQ, frequently achieving value from the investment in data science.

Data team freedom

Finally, in a data-driven culture, the data team has the freedom and resources to do what it has been hired to do. It's free to experiment, and there are little or no restrictions on data access for BAs and DSs. The data team has access to an adequate sandbox (a place to experiment and try things out), allowing them to store and process memory-intensive, large and frequently changing amounts of data.

THE PATH TO A DATA-DRIVEN ORGANISATION

Some organisations are data driven from their inception – they have it in their DNA. Others can only achieve success through a process of behaviour change.

Companies such as Google and Facebook were all founded by engineers. The founders, Larry Page and Mark Zuckerberg respectively, have strong computing backgrounds and, as a result, they are inclined to find uses for the increasing insights that can be generated by data. Other technology companies share the same traits. For example, LinkedIn, Netflix and Amazon all use algorithmically generated insights from the PYMK (people you may know) algorithm, used in their content and product recommendation engines. For organisations like these, the environmental conditions are perfect for generating value from big data.

Other companies – particularly those that are older, less technical or have succeeded in the past without the explicit need for data science – tend not to adapt so easily to data-driven behaviour. Instead, they will have to go through an intentional change programme to create the optimal environment for success.

The good news is that this is change is possible, even in the most extreme circumstances, because cultures are not static; they are dynamic and can change in response to external and internal changes. A common example is found in the book by Michael Lewis, *Moneyball: The Art of Winning an Unfair Game*.[9] The game of baseball has been around for over 150 years, and during most of that time, team management has followed traditional methods of gauging players, identifying prospects and even deciding on in-game strategies, based almost exclusively on the intuition of scouts and team management.

However, Billy Beane, general manager of the Oakland Athletics, ignored these traditional methods and began using an analytical, evidence-based approach to the game under extreme financial constraints relative to other baseball teams. He used data, analytics and statistical analysis to determine who to recruit for the team, what each player should do once on the field and even determine which strategic tactics the team should employ for each game.

---

9 Lewis, M (2004) *Moneyball: The Art of Winning an Unfair Game*, New York, WW Norton & Company.

Beane and his team were able to demonstrate that the traditional approach was subjective, outdated and often flawed – much to the initial disdain of his colleagues in the major leagues. He built a data-driven culture within his team that resulted in such phenomenal success that all other teams in the league now follow the same approach.

This story serves as a highly instructive example of what to expect when embarking on organisational change to build a data culture. Its popularity and corresponding success have even led to the use of term 'moneyball' as a verb to describe organisations that use data and have been successful. There are a growing number of examples of companies that have made this cultural shift and 'moneyballed' their organisations and industries.

Ultimately, moving towards a data-driven culture is a process of working with people and technology to change behaviour. In his book *Sapiens*, Yuval Noah Harari says that culture is a network of artificial instincts that make us think in a certain way, behave according to certain standards, want certain things and observe certain rules. This illustrates that it's all about behaviour, and there are three dimensions of organisational culture that drive the resulting behaviours. It begins with symbolic reminders (artefacts that are entirely visible), keystone behaviours (recurring acts that trigger other behaviours and that are both visible and invisible) and mindsets (attitudes and beliefs that are widely shared but are exclusively invisible).

Behaviours are the most powerful determinant of real change. What people do matters more than what they say or believe. Therefore, to move to a more data-driven culture, you should start working on changing the most critical behaviours – and the mindsets will follow. Over time, altered behaviour patterns and habits can produce better results.

For example, consider BJ Fogg's 'Behavior Model'. The model states that, for a new target behaviour to be adopted, you need three principal factors:

1. Enough motivation

2. Enough ability

3. An effective trigger

All three factors must be present at the same time for the desired behaviour change to occur.

Motivation

Dr Edward Deci, Professor of Psychology at the University of Rochester, defines motivation as the 'energy for action'. Motivation is essentially the level of desire for a behaviour. While the nature of motivation is a widely contested topic in psychology, BJ Fogg states that there are three core motivators that propel our desire to act. We are motivated by our senses to seek pleasure and avoid pain, by our anticipation to hope instead of fear, and social cohesion to secure social acceptance or rejection. An increase in pleasure, hope and social acceptance increases motivation, while an increase in pain, fear and rejection is likely to decrease it.

Culture is powerfully shaped by incentives. The best predictor of what people will do is what they are incentivised to do. Incentives can include monetary rewards, non-monetary rewards (such as status, recognition and advancement) and sanctions – to which all members of the organisation are subject. The leadership team should take time to incentivise and reward behaviour that conforms with a data-driven culture.

Ability

In short, anything that can be done to reduce the steps or the number of tasks in any process will increase the chances of its adoption. If you want the business to benefit from informed decisions, employees need the ability to easily find, understand and use the data. The simpler this is, the more likely it is that they will adopt the behaviours desired. To provide this ability effectively and make data simple to use, the following points must be considered:

Time

If a target behaviour requires time and we don't have time available, then the behaviour is not simple. For example, if I'm routinely asked to fill out an online form that has 100 fields in it, I'm not likely to complete the form because it's not simple for me and I have other demands on my time.

Physical effort

Behaviours that require physical effort may not be seen as simple. For example, if I want to see statistics on the types of customer support calls we've had over the last year but the records are kept in the hot storeroom of our satellite office, I'm probably not going to retrieve them. I'll make a guess based on my experience and gut feeling instead.

Brain cycles

If performing a target behaviour causes us to think hard, that might not be simple. This is especially true if our minds are occupied by other issues. We tend to overestimate how much people in general want to think; thinking deeply or thinking in new ways can be difficult for many.

Social deviance

If a target behaviour requires me to be socially irregular, then that behaviour is no longer simple. For example, wearing pyjamas to a city council meeting might require little effort, but there's a social price I'd pay, which creates complications for that behaviour.

Routine

In seeking simplicity, people will often stick to their routine, like buying petrol at the same station, even if it costs more money or takes more time than other options, since it's familiar to them. Anything that requires action outside of routine is not simple.

Another important contributor to enabling ability is getting the big data and business teams to speak the same language. I've found cross-training and collaboration to be successful in achieving this.

Once your team is in position, cross-training is critical. For example, I came across a company in the insurance space that intentionally spent time training their analysts on insurance and business users on analytics. The goal was not to make everyone an expert on everything, but to establish a common language that the group could use to collaborate effectively.

Enabling team members to trade places also helped ensure that the group shared a vested interest in the success of the outcome. In addition, it exposed each of the team members to different work cultures. Don't forget the importance of designing incentive structures that foster brainstorming and building a collective mindset.

Trigger

The last factor needed to change behaviour is a trigger or something that tells people to perform a behaviour now. Often overlooked or taken for granted, triggers are vital. In fact, with behaviours for which people have enough motivation and ability – a trigger is all that's required. Hiring a data owner in a senior position is a strong way to send a signal to the rest of the organisation that data is important, and is usually a sufficient trigger to effect behaviour change. Other triggers include regularly scheduled data reviews, scheduled reminders or meetings to review the latest data results, and requiring data-driven information in weekly status reports.

Once you understand the employee characteristics and organisational structure of data-driven organisation, it becomes easier to enact the motivation, enablers and triggers described here to put your own company on the path to becoming data driven and reaping the game-changing results we've been talking about. It can be a challenge, but it's worth the effort!

Concluding Thoughts

There's much to absorb from all the information presented in this book. The most important thing to understand is that, while there is fantastic opportunity in data, it's not easy to achieve.

There are many moving parts, misconceptions and misused terminology that make it incredibly difficult to successfully implement a big-data solution. You can't execute steps to successfully solve the data puzzle without a comprehensive understanding of the fundamentals of what data can do for you, what it means and how it's used in organisations to recognise and realise value.

Despite these difficulties, organisations should not risk standing on the sidelines; the potential impact of not getting involved can be catastrophic.

My hope is that readers can put this book down having gained the notion that big data is nothing more than data – it's just that there is so much more of it, and in so many different varieties, being produced at such a high rate. It's big data's popular cousin – data science – that deals with the process of delivering value from big data. This process itself has many moving parts and many skills required to get it to work. Searching for the mythical DS that 'does it all' is a fruitless exercise. Instead, organisations should take time to build the right team, fill the right roles and find the relevant skill sets.

Organisations need to appoint their data leader carefully. They are in a critical position to make these projects a success or failure, and for that they must sit together with senior leadership. If data (big or small) is essentially meant to improve the quality of decisions that an organisation or its customers make, then positioning them anywhere else will greatly limit their chance of success. Moreover, organisational culture is one of the leading keys to success, and they won't be able to influence culture from anywhere other than a C-suite position.

As with any other senior role, your data leader will need support throughout the process as they create their data game plan, recruit for their team and oversee their activities in the organisation.

Organisations should resist overcomplicating the process of finding use cases. Since realising value from data comes from using it to make better decisions, time should be invested in understanding what key decisions are needed, how they impact core metrics and which ones would be ideal candidates for big-data use cases. Once prioritised, the team can then begin the process of execution with the best chance of success.

Finally, this book should serve as a regular point of reference. Keep it to hand and refer to it when your data efforts appear to stumble or a piece of the puzzle seems to be missing. Share it with your colleagues. There's a lot to take in, and much of it can only become second nature through experience and iterative execution.

I wish you success in cracking the data code for your organisation.

Acknowledgements

The world is a better place, we are healthier and safer thanks to people who want to harness the power of data. Thank you to everyone who strives to understand data, get it to work and use it to help your organisations and to help others.

Turning your hypothesis, thoughts, experiments and results into a book is as hard as it sounds. The experience is both challenging and rewarding. I especially want to thank the people who helped make this happen.

I have to start by thanking my awesome wife, Delina. From dealing with my moods to keeping our three beautiful children busy whilst I was working on the book, you were always there for me. Without your love and support, there is no way that this book would have been finished. To my children, Joshua, Caleb and Isaiah, my parents, my siblings and my HOME church family, thank you for your ever present emotional and spiritual support. You will stand as the most influential group of people I will ever know, and each of you have contributed in your own way to the man I am today. Thank you.

Those friends of mine who have I have talked with about this journey, laughed with and broke bread with, you know who you are and the part that you played. Thank you. Nicole Tache, you were so encouraging throughout the process; our conference calls always left me energised to tackle the next section. My friends who took time to review the book, Richard Atkinson, Karol Ussher and Neil Staunton – my proofreaders, concept testers and sounding boards. I am also really grateful for all of your valuable feedback! Claire Grove, thank you for getting me to talk about this on stage at the big conferences and in front of the camera. David Reed, thank you for adding me into your network and introducing me to the many other chief data officers out there today, each of them adding further justification to the content in this book. You have all helped shape the book into what it is today. Thank you.

Finally, without the experiences and support from my peers and team at JustGiving this book would not exist. You have given me the opportunity to lead a great group of individuals – I was blessed to be a leader of such gifted people who have used data to grow the world of generosity, raising billions for great causes. Thank you to Liz K, Paul O, Leo, Richard, Sian,

Simon, Mike U, Antonios, Ben, Ivo, Tomas, Stephen, Olly, Ted, Alkesh, Debs T, Raven, Panda and Koala. I also want to thank each member of the management team and the board. Zarine and Anne-Marie, thank you for inviting me on to the team; Anna K, Charlie and Andy, thank you for listening. I especially have to acknowledge Bela Hatvany. Thank you for being one of the best listeners that I have met. The ability to hear people even when they do not speak is a rare gift, and on many occasions you were the only one who heard me. Thank you.

The Author

Mike is an entrepreneur, author and international speaker. His experience and passion for working with data and analytics began at university in the late 1990s when he discovered the predictive power of signal processing and regression. Combining this with his childhood passion for computer programming he quickly found himself in a career that required him to work with databases, software engineering and mathematical algorithms to solve business problems.

As a consultant in the data space, Mike has worked with organisations across a range of industries from fintech and health to non-profits and government agencies. He has primarily advised leaders on how to create optimised data science teams, created data cultures, written data strategies and assessed how organisations can generate real business value with data.

Mike cites his time at JustGiving as one of his big recent achievements, where he built a team that worked with data to build AI algorithms to unlock generosity and raise millions for charities in the process. His work quickly got him recognition as one of the UK's top digital masters, resulting in regular invites to give keynotes for large organisations like Microsoft and a host of other conferences around the world. He has won several awards and has been named as one of the most influential people in a data-driven business in the UK over the last few years.

Mike has also spearheaded some work on the interplay between data and behavioural economics, essentially researching the role data plays in human behaviours and choices. This has proven to be very interesting to researchers and companies that work with large consumer audiences, resulting in guest lectures and speaking invitations to a range of well-known institutions including Harvard University.

Much of his work can be found in technical magazines, press articles and a couple of recent bestselling big data books.

Find out more about Mike, or contact him, via:

www.thedatacode.com

www.mikebugembe.com

www.twitter.com/mikebugembe

www.linkedin.com/in/mikebugembe

www.instagram.com/mikebugembe

Printed in Great Britain
by Amazon